PATHWAYS TO SPIRITUALITY

ALSO BY BILL O'HANLON

A Guide to Inclusive Therapy

A Brief Guide to Brief Therapy
(with Brian Cade)

A Guide to Possibility Land
(with Sandy Beadle)

An Uncommon Casebook
(with Angela Hexum)

Even From a Broken Web
(with Bob Bertolino)

In Search of Solutions
(with Michele Weiner-Davis)

Stop Blaming, Start Loving
(with Pat Hudson)

Rewriting Love Stories
(with Pat Hudson)

Solution-Oriented Hypnosis
(with Michael Martin)

Taproots

PATHWAYS TO SPIRITUALITY

Connection, Wholeness, and Possibility
for Therapist and Client

BILL O'HANLON

W. W. NORTON & COMPANY
NEW YORK · LONDON

For information about permission to reproduce
selections from this book, write to Permissions, W. W. Norton
& Company, Inc., 500 Fifth Avenue, New York, NY 10110

Manufacturing by Haddon Craftsmen
Book design by Charlotte Staub
Production Manager: Leeann Graham

Library of Congress Cataloging-in-Publication Data

O'Hanlon, William Hudson.
  Pathways to spirituality : connection, wholeness,
and possibility for therapist and client / by Bill
O'Hanlon.
     p. cm.
  Includes bibliographical references and index.
  ISBN 0-393-70489-0
     1. Psychotherapy—Religious aspects. 2. Spiritual
healing. 3. Spirituality. I. Title.

RC489.S676064 2006
616.89'14—dc22   2005052340

W. W. Norton & Company, Inc.,
500 Fifth Avenue, New York, N.Y. 10110

www.wwnorton.com

W. W. Norton & Company Ltd.,
Castle House, 75/76 Wells St., London W1T 3QT

0 2 4 6 8 9 7 5 3 1

For Steffanie,
for the love and loyalty and
for challenging me to bring more of
myself to my work and my life.
You are my connection.

For Biscuit,
my nonhuman connection.
You sweet crazy flying squirrel boy.

For Patrick,
in hopes of future
reconnections.

To God.
It all begins and ends with you
(and Paracletes—thanks
for the words).

CONTENTS

Acknowledgments

BIANCA SIVAN, my assistant, for the support needed to be able to write. She takes care of the details, something I'm not very good at.

Martha Geske, my former assistant, who died during the planning and conception of this book. You are missed and our prayers are with you.

The team from Norton Professional Books, Deborah Malmud, Michael McGandy, Kevin Olsen, and Andrea Costella. Thanks for all your work on making this book a reality.

Participants in my workshops on spirituality and therapy, who asked the right questions and made suggestions for improvement of this material. And many of whom also encouraged me to write this book.

Gary Bonalumi and Sandy Beadle, for their unpaid but greatly valuable help with research.

The city of Florence, Italy, for the fine weather that facilitated the completion of this manuscript. Long walks through your narrow streets helped me process all this material unconsciously. Your city is infused with spirituality. Ciao, bella.

PATHWAYS TO SPIRITUALITY

Why Spirituality in Therapy?

❄

THROUGH THE YEARS, as I have been teaching work-shops on my approach to therapy, more times than I can count someone has walked up to me during a break and asked, "You're spiritual, aren't you?" I was initially sur-prised by this query, since I did not mention anything about spirituality in my presentations. The questioners routinely responded that they had heard the spirituality "between the lines."

I finally decided to create a seminar that would speak to the topic of spirituality and therapy. I never believed that my clients (or anyone else's for that matter) were defined or determined only by their symptoms, their childhoods and

1

family background, their biology or genetics, or their psychology. I have always had the sense that there is not only more to people, but resources beyond the individual and beyond humans that can help people move out of being stuck.

As I sought out books, articles, and tapes to help me articulate how spirituality could be integrated into therapy, I was frustrated because none of these materials really spoke to my sense of the subject. So I began to explore the topic through a series of workshops on integrating spirituality into therapy. The workshops I have done for the past few years helped me develop my own way of articulating and clarifying how to use spirituality in therapy without being impositional.

Workshop participants began to ask, "When are you going to write a book on this?" I told them I usually write the book when the workshop stops shifting around so much and I get clear on what I have to say. That time has come. I am passionate about the importance of integrating spirituality into the therapy process. I began to develop the sense, after doing many workshops on the topic, that I had something that was immediately accessible to therapists and was clear and powerful. Here's the book. You can decide for yourself.

It is important to bring spirituality into therapy because our clients often do and to leave it out would not only be disrespectful, but wasteful. Most people in the United States profess a belief in God and attach importance to religion. A Gallup poll taken in 1997 showed that 61% of the respondents said that religion was "very important" in their lives; 27% answered "fairly important." That means that almost 90% of the people who come to see U.S. therapists have a sense that religion is significant in their lives (Gallup, 1998).

Beyond that, as I will make the case in this book, spirituality holds resources that can rapidly help people get unstuck or cope with their therapy-related troubles.

SPIRITUALITY BLOCKS

If one looks to the origins of the word *psychotherapy*, one finds it comes from two roots, *psyche*, which in the Greek means "soul," and *therapy*, which in Greek means something akin to "healing" or "treating." So psychotherapy originally referred to "soul healing." How did we get so far away from this sense of working with and healing the soul, instead focusing on working with the mind, emotions, thoughts, and so on? And why, although there were some pioneers and advocates over the years like Frankl (1997), Jung (1955), and Assagioli (2000), who stressed the importance of spirituality for mental health, did therapy generally disdain or discourage using spirituality or spiritual methods for so long?

There are several sources for this reluctance or parting of the ways, in my view.

The first is Freud's hostility or disdain for religion. His father was very religious and Freud rejected this sensibility in his life. He expressed views that held that religion was a defense mechanism and a neurosis. Religious ideas, he wrote, "are illusions, fulfillments of the oldest, strongest and most urgent wishes of mankind," and religion is "the universal obsessional neurosis of humanity" (1927/1961, pp. 30, 43). Not a very supportive view, to say the least! Given the enormous influence Freud had on the first 100 years of therapy (this effect is waning more recently), it is not surprising that this had a restraining effect on the use of spirituality or religion as a resource in therapy.

Behaviorism came next as a major influence on therapy and psychology. Behaviorism, at least at first, attempted to banish any internal experience, including spirituality, as being part of the unknowable "black box." Behaviorists also sought to make psychology more scientific, which meant distancing itself from the vague and hard-to-investigate area of spirituality.

Many therapists have less interest or belief in religion or God than the average client. There is evidence that about 75% of Americans say that religion influences every facet their life, but only 32% of psychiatrists, 33% of clinical psychologists, and 46% of social workers say the same (Paul, 2005). According to an American Association of Pastoral Counselors/Samaritan Centers jointly sponsored poll of Americans conducted by Greenberg Quinlan Research in October 2000, 83% of respondents felt that their spiritual faith and religious beliefs were closely tied to their state of mental and emotional health. Among

African-American respondents, virtually all (97%) held this view. There is a mismatch with therapy and therapists here. In a survey done with marriage and family therapists in 2002, Carlson (2002) found that 96% of them thought there was a relationship between spirituality and mental health, but only 62% of these same therapists said that they thought spiritual issues should be considered in clinical work. Neelman and King's (1993) survey of 200 London psychiatrists found that 90% viewed religious beliefs as relevant to patient mental health, but few knew how to bring religious beliefs into clinical work.

The next restraining influence is that therapists are often told that bringing spirituality or religion into the therapy context involves imposing one's beliefs on clients or patients. This is a legitimate concern we are going to deal with in this book. In fact, I might say that this is almost the purpose of this book—to show a way to bring spirituality into therapy without imposing.

When I take surveys about this in my workshops, about a third of therapists attending tell me that they were given warnings not to bring spirituality or religion into their clinical work, about a third got the message that it was okay or even important to do so, and about a third didn't get a message one way or the other in their training, schooling, or supervision. (Bringing spirituality into therapy has little to do with having people kneel down and pray to Jesus during sessions, as some therapists or supervisors fear. More on that later.)

Another barrier to bringing spirituality into therapy is the lack of a clear or practical definition of spirituality. The core of this book rests on a simple and useful definition, which provides guidelines for accessing spirituality without being impositional. Part of my frustration when reading other books on this subject was the lack of a clear definition of spirituality. It was almost as though the authors were afraid of being definitive, again for fear of imposing. One workshop presenter I heard did offer a definitive statement: "Spirituality," he declared, "is creativity and joy!" Definitive but not helpful, in my view. Without a clear and accessible definition, therapists lack direction to bringing this resource and sensibility into clinical work.

SPIRITUALITY VERSUS RELIGION

This is a book about spirituality and therapy, not religion and therapy. While there is much to be admired about religion (and indeed, much to disapprove of at times), the focus here is exclusively on spirituality. For more on the admirable and important aspects of religion that may be missing from therapy, see Chapter 5.

Religion refers to a specific set of beliefs and practices. So, for instance, Buddhism is clearly different from Southern Baptism, and Islam is easy to distinguish from Mormonism on the basis of the rituals one performs and the beliefs one espouses in each of these religions.

There are many problems with bringing religion into therapy that can be avoided with a more spiritual approach. Even if one's client is of the same religion, differences in the practice and interpretation of that particular religion's tenets can lead to difficulties.

In researching the material for this book, I was surprised to learn that until fairly recently, religion was viewed as the more inclusive, larger concept in which spirituality was contained. But in modern times, spirituality has come to be seen as the broader concept. Some people feel alienated by or hostile toward religion. (Fewer seem to be hostile toward spirituality, except for those who equate spirituality with New Age beliefs and who have objections to this New Age view of the world.) In a poll commissioned by *Spirituality and Health* magazine (2000), it was found that 59% of respondents described themselves as both spiritual and religious, 65% had positive associations with the word *religion* (15% found it negative), and 74% had positive associations with the word *spirituality* (6% found it negative).

In this book, we will generally confine ourselves to the topic of spirituality, in order to be inclusive and to avoid doctrinaire difficulties. *Spirituality* is a sense that there is something bigger going on in life. We will expand and specify this definition soon. *Religion*, on the other hand, involves specific beliefs and practices.

This approach, like all others to therapy, rests on certain assumptions. Please keep in mind these are only starting points that I recommend you hold loosely and not get too attached to, but they give some sort of structure to help inform the approach put forth in this book. To make these assumptions explicit so you can examine whether they fit for you and your clients, I have listed them below. They seem to me fairly obvious, so I have merely listed them and not expanded on them here. The rest of the book will expand upon many of them and give more details on why I hold them and how they might be helpful in the therapy process.

- Religion is distinct from spirituality for some people.
- People are not defined by or determined by the circumstances of their lives. There is more to people than nature or nurture, personality, genetics, biochemistry, or cause and effect.
- People have spiritual resources, even when they are not religious or when they profess no spiritual sensibilities or beliefs.
- Therapists can bring a spiritual sensibility into therapy without imposing it on clients.
- People have already developed ways of tapping into a sense of something bigger than themselves.
- Drawing on spiritual resources can facilitate therapy outcomes.
- Spirituality is a central or meaningful part of a majority of our clients' lives. To leave it out of psychotherapy is as much a disservice as imposing spirituality on them.

THE VALUE OF SPIRITUALITY AND RELIGION IN MENTAL HEALTH

There is a great deal of research pointing to the likelihood that having spiritual or religious beliefs or practices can have a beneficial effect in preventing or recovering from common behavioral, emotional, psychological, addictive, or relational problems. We will examine some of this research in a later section. Because this is mainly a clinical book, we won't spend as much time on this area as could be spent, but the reader will at least know that, although this area is fairly new in therapy, there is some research support for using it.

There is also a great deal of research on the correlation between religious practices, religious sensibilities, and spiritual sensibilities with various aspects of mental and behavioral health, but a few cautions must be noted about this research. One is that this is a relatively new area of research, only really beginning in the late 1980s in earnest and only recently picking up steam (and funding). The second is that much of this research is correlational. That is, religious practices and sensibilities seem to be related to positive effects in the areas of mental and emotional health. (This is true for the most part; we will detail some of the exceptions to this rule.) There is very little experimental/causal research, although, again, more has recently emerged. Still, like the correlational research that exists between smoking and lung cancer, I would not be inclined to wait until the causal links are proven beyond a shadow of a doubt to stop smoking, even though this decision rests on shaky scientific grounds at the moment. Having said that, let's press on.

The best source of research information in this area is contained in the massive volume compiled by Koenig, McCullough, and Larson (2001). Another comprehensive review is Levin (2001).

The research is actually too much to cover in this small volume and mostly concerns religion, but I will summarize it simply this way: having religious or spiritual sensibilities, beliefs, or practices is generally correlated with preventive or positive effects on a wide range of mental, behavioral, emotional, and relational issues. These include such areas as depression, anxiety, major mental illness, drug and alcohol abuse and dependency, marital stability, and delinquency. Note that I wrote that it is *generally* correlated; there are a few exceptions.

And now, in the next section, we will take up a simple, clear definition of spirituality that will give us access to it in therapy without imposing.

SPIRITUALITY: THE 3 CS

When I say spirituality, I don't necessarily mean religion; I mean whatever it is that helps you feel connected to something that is larger than yourself. —DEAN ORNISH, M.D.

So, here it is, my simple definition of spirituality. It has three components that I think encompass almost everything that religion and spiritual approaches have in common. This definition is also useful in that it gives clear guidelines for how to access spirituality in therapy (and in life). Those three components, which I call the 3 Cs, are:

1. CONNECTION, that is, when people feel connected to something beyond their petty, little selves (or egos). Spirituality refers to what is beyond the "little self," or the personality. Anything that gives one an experience of the "bigger self," or what is beyond the limited personality, can be a component of spirituality. We will detail seven typical areas in which people feel connected to that something bigger to expand on this element of spirituality.

2. COMPASSION. This is the place where we can feel kindness or acceptance toward others, and there is a softening of the usual mistrust, harshness, or judgmental attitude we feel. It's a sense of "feeling with" rather than being against self, others, or the world.

3. CONTRIBUTION OR SERVICE. Usually this comes out of the first two Cs. When we feel connected to something beyond our petty, selfish selves, and when we feel compassion, we are usually moved to make a contribution to others and to the world and to be of service.

When people seek therapy, they are often feeling isolated, disconnected and disempowered, at least in some area of their lives. Spirituality, in this definition, begins with the opposite of this experience. It is a movement to-

ward feeling connected to something bigger within or beyond oneself that can evoke feelings of competence or
okayness.

The rest of this book will be an expansion of these
three basic ideas, with some side issues thrown in to en-
rich the journey. Next, we take up the idea of connection
in more detail.

CHAPTER ONE

Seven Pathways to Connection

Only connect.
—E.M. FORSTER

HERE IS A LIST of seven possible pathways to help people connect with that something bigger within or beyond themselves. (Incidentally, the word *religion* derives from Latin *religare*, which means "to reconnect.") Any one may work. Some may not work for or appeal to some people. What I like about this list is that some of these pathways do not sound like religious or even spiritual concepts to most people, thereby bypassing any negative reactions people might have if they have antipathy or trauma associated with religion or spirituality. As long as they avoid any spiritual or religious phrasing in asking about or investigating these pathways, therapists can usually access this area without triggering any reactions. Obviously, though, if clients profess spiritual or religious sensibilities, therapists need not tread so carefully.

THE SEVEN PATHWAYS

1. Connection to the Soul, the Deeper Self, the Spirit

This is connection to the deepest level within and involves having a connection with oneself that is beyond the rational, logical, or even the emotional. Many people find that meditating, journaling, or just spending time alone helps them find this connection.

I had a client who was suffering from the aftereffects of sexual abuse. She found it hard to connect with her own experience and often did not know what she was thinking or feeling for hours or even days after she thought or felt it. She developed a habit of writing in a journal in her locked room (so she felt safe) each night and began to recognize her experience sooner and more frequently.

2. Connection to or through the Body

This connection may come through dancing, sex, athletics, yoga, eating fine foods, and so on. Seeing Michael Jordan in the air about to make a basket or other great athletes in action can show the spiritual through the body—they seem to do things that are beyond usual human abilities and that seem transcendent. Athletes often speak of being "in the zone," a spiritual-like state of effortless and unselfconscious performance. People can also connect to the body by attending to sensual experiences—the proverbial stopping to smell the roses. Eating slowly and really savoring the food is another example of this pathway.

A client of mine who had been sexually abused told me that she didn't really have a sense of where her body was most of the time and therefore was forever running into things and bruising herself. Together we came up with a two-pronged plan for reconnecting her to her body. First, she agreed to stand naked in front of a mirror for 15 minutes every night for 2 weeks, examining her body without judgment or criticism. She was just to notice it and notice how it changed when she moved or changed positions. Next, she contacted a massage therapist she knew and explained that she had been sexually abused and found it excruciatingly painful and embarrassing to be touched. The massage therapist agreed to proceed slowly, and they gradually worked her into getting full body massages, which both relieved a lot of muscle tension and reconnected her to her body.

3. Connection to Another Being

This refers to intimate one-on-one relationships, what philosopher Martin Buber (1971) called the I-Thou relationship. This pathway does not always need to refer to a relationship with another person; it could be with an animal. For example, a client of mine who was suicidal told me that the only thing that kept her alive was her connection with her dog. She knew that the dog needed her and that no one would love the dog like she did.

A well-known adolescent therapist, Ron Taffel, used what he called the "second family" of the adolescent when he couldn't develop a connection with the teen in therapy or between the teen and the teen's family (2002). The term *second family* refers to teen clients' best friends. Taffel often found that teens listened to and were influenced by these close friends, even though it seemed they were beyond reach. Even when the teens were not connected to their families, there *were* connected to their best friends (their "second family").

I often ask couples I work with to tell me about times and activities in which they have felt most connected to each other and then suggest that they do that activity to reevoke that time. One couple, with a stressful schedule and a 1-year-old, talked about how they used to take walks together. They put the baby in the stroller and began to walk every evening, talking and reconnecting.

4. Connection to Community

This pathway involves one's relationship to family, extended family, neighborhood, church group, movement, or workplace. Research has shown that clients' perceptions of increased social support outside of the treatment relationship were more important in terms of symptom reduction than growth in the strength of the therapeutic alliance (Mallinckrodt, 1996).

Group therapy and support groups can be means of creating community connections for disconnected clients.

Sometimes these group connections can be harmful or lead to violence, for example, membership in a gang or nationalistic or ethnic loyalties that can lead to ethnic cleansings—so we will be careful to temper this one with the other two Cs, compassion and contribution.

5. Connection through Nature

This pathway is about being in and noticing nature and the physical environment. "I believe in God, only I spell it Nature," said Frank Lloyd Wright (Harris, 2005). One may also experience this sense of connection through a deep understanding and appreciation of the laws of nature, such as physics and mathematics. (Being a liberal arts major, I think I'll stick with mountains and forests and lakes for my nature connection.)

Howard Frumkin, M.D. (Frumkin, 2001), wrote a nice summary article of the various positive effects that being connected to nature had on people in different settings. They include:

• Patients with rooms overlooking deciduous trees healed more quickly and had less need for pain medication than patients who viewed a brick wall.

- Dental patients who stared at a large mural of a natural scene had lower blood pressure and less anxiety than those who didn't.
- Inmates whose cell windows face the prison yard made 24% more sick-call visits than those whose cells looked outward on rolling farmland and trees.

My Australian friend and colleague George Burns investigated the positive effects of connecting to nature in treating mental health issues (Burns, 1998). His book also includes research as well as some methods for bringing nature connections into therapy as resources and interventions. I remember one intervention he used. A couple was arguing on a regular basis. Dr. Burns suggested that they have the same discussion walking through a local forest. The discussion went much differently, just because they were in a different setting.

6. Connection by Participating in, Creating, or Appreciating Art

Some people are moved to tears when looking at a painting in a museum. Others feel energized or moved when listening to a piece of music. Depending on one's preferences, this sense of connection to something bigger may come through literature, painting, sculpture, theater, movies, photography, or dance. Many artists refer to a sense that they are not making the art they produce, but that it is coming to or through them from some place beyond or bigger than themselves.

A therapist had a client who was a painter. The client was stuck and hadn't been able to paint for years. The therapist asked the client to make him a gift of a painting in lieu of a fee for one session. The client was to paint whatever picture came, not worrying about the quality of it and was to call it "Blocked." The client brought it in to the therapist and told him that he had begun painting again once he finished the therapist's painting. The therapist got up and threw the "Blocked" painting in his fireplace and burned it, saying, "That's the end of Blocked."

Joyce Mills, Richard Crowley, and Margaret Ryan (1986/ 2001) used a technique with children in which they would have them draw a picture of where they were now (the problem) and then draw a rainbow bridge to another image of where they would like to be. On the bridge, they would put whatever resources they would need to make it over the bridge. This often helped the therapist and the child clients to create solutions.

7. Connection to the Universe, Higher Power, God, or Cosmic Consciousness

Whatever word one uses for the sense that there is a greater being or intelligence than ourselves at work in life, this connection can happen through prayer, conversion, meditating, reading the sacred works of the religion one prefers, and so on.

The beginnings of Alcoholics Anonymous show this element. A man who was drinking episodically was in therapy with Carl Jung. After his latest binge, he despaired in his therapy session. He asked Jung if he could do anything to stop these binges, as they were destroying his life. Jung replied that honestly, he didn't think that therapy could help a person like his client. The client was discouraged and asked Jung what he thought would work. Jung said that the only thing he'd ever seen work in such cases was conversion to a religion. The client asked sarcastically, "Great, how can I implement that?" Jung replied calmly that if it were he, he would attend any and all revivals until one "took." The client actually followed the plan, and finally one "took." He attended a revival at Madison Square Garden put on by the Oxford Society, found Jesus, and got sober. Through a series of connections, the story of this success spread to other people who had trouble with alcohol, including the founders of AA.

I actually came across this pathway some years ago when I had a client who became frightened during a session. My supervisor had explicitly told me never to bring in spiritual issues in therapy, but when I asked the client what might help her feel safer, she said that imagining that Jesus was putting his hand on her shoulder would be comforting. When I looked around, I didn't see my supervisor there, so I encouraged her to go ahead and imagine that. She calmed down and we went on with the session. I thought about it and decided that it would have been more impositional to leave out this resource than to bring it in. If I had introduced this idea, it would, of course, had been impositional on my part.

ASSESSING THE SEVEN PATHWAYS TO CONNECTION

Some of our clients have such an antipathy toward spirituality or religion that asking questions with anything that sounds religious or spiritual would be off-putting. One of the things I like about these pathways is that they don't sound like spiritual questions to most clients, since they are not thinking about spirituality in terms of the "connection to something bigger within or beyond you" definition I have offered here. Here are some questions that fit in with my definition that still get to the idea of connecting with something bigger within or beyond the individual. Use these or your own variations for these clients. And then again, you might just listen for spontaneous reports of places or times where people are connected during the clinical conversation.

- How do you typically connect to something bigger within or beyond you?
- How do you connect with your deeper self?
- How do you connect with or get in touch with your body?
- How do you connect deeply with others?

- What places or times in nature are the best for you?
- What is your favorite art form or activity?
- What are the times and ways you have felt the most expansive or experienced a sense of awe?
- What music has touched your soul the most deeply?
- If you were to create a personal retreat place, where would it be located?
- What book would you say has most touched your soul?
- Who do you feel most connected to?
- What group do you feel most a part of?

Another way you might use these pathways is to notice or investigate where your client is disconnected. We will discuss how to reconnect people in a later section.

ESTABLISHING CONNECTION

A number of strategies and tools exist to help your clients create and maintain these seven areas of connection.

Rituals

Therapists can help clients develop or restore rituals of connection. These are rituals that help clients make a connection in any of the seven pathways. Often clients have already developed these rituals but some life changes or traumas have disrupted the clients' use of them. Therapists need to discover the rituals their clients have used and help them restore or change them slightly to update the connection rituals to current situations.

Glenn (1989) showed that children from families in which one or both parents were abusing drugs did better as adults when their rituals were kept intact. What do I mean by "did better as adults" and by "keeping their rituals intact"? Glenn compared children who grew up in these families, often with a lot of stress, often physical or emotional abuse, neglect, and so on, and found that some of them didn't develop the problems as adults that most of them did. That is, they didn't develop drug or alcohol problems themselves, or become depressed or anxious, or develop criminal behaviors. What was the difference in the two groups? In the more resilient ones, the ones who did better, it was discovered that in at least some areas of their lives, they had some sense of connection and stability because they participated in some recurring activity that was positive (or at least neutral) and that connected them with themselves, others, God, nature, art, or any of the other of the seven pathways to connection detailed in the previous section.

I grew up in a large Irish Catholic family (eight kids) and there were a few things I could always count on in my family. One was that everyone gathered around the table at dinnertime each night at the same time (6 P.M. sharp!). This was our time to connect with one another, to discuss how our days had gone, to exchange information, jokes, stories, food, and so on. One had to have a very good reason not to be there, but we wouldn't have wanted to miss it anyway. Another ritual was going to church. We went as a family every Sunday morning, getting dressed up in our Sunday best.

There were other rituals: holidays, like Thanksgiving and Easter and Christmas. All had repetitive themes and activities one could anticipate that felt familiar and comforting. Birthdays also had a similar structure, involving singing the birthday song twice (at the urging of my father, who would say after the first go-round, "Once more with gusto") and the donning of a paper crown to signify that the birthday boy or girl was king or queen for the day.

In the families cited in Glenn (1989), those whose rituals were torn or missing did poorly as adults. Those who had at least some of these repetitive activities did much better as adults. There seems to be something stabilizing and comforting and connective in having repeating activities that connect time and people and environments.

If clients have had connective rituals in the past, but something has disrupted them or the clients have just fallen out of the habit, therapists' tasks may be as simple as reminding clients and encouraging them to take up these rituals again. But circumstances may have changed and therapists may need to help clients make variations on the old rituals to restore them. For example, a woman I worked with in therapy had a ritual every evening of running in the park near her home, but this ritual had been disrupted when someone grabbed her while she was running and tried to wrestle her into the bushes in an attempted rape. She fought back and yelled and people nearby heard her distress and came to help. The attacker ran off and the woman stopped her evening run through the park. She missed the green trees and the time alone to decompress. After some discussion, she decided that she would run every other day with a friend; on alternate days, she would run on a treadmill while listening to motivational tapes, which she enjoyed but rarely had time to do in her busy life. These rituals weren't the same as her previous ritual, but they served to connect her to her body, to another person, and to herself. She would have to discover a new way to connect to nature.

At times, clients do not really have any rituals, and therapists can help them create rituals of connection. For example, a client of mine had been raised in a chaotic household. Meals were "catch as catch can," meaning family members got or made their own food and ate whenever or wherever they wanted. My client was feeling as if the same thing was happening in her own family, with her husband coming home late from work many nights and the kids eating dinner on TV trays in the living room while watching TV. We discussed how she envied her friends who had more structure when she was growing up, especially when their families ate dinner all together. She had a talk with her husband and kids, who agreed to try a monthlong experiment in eating in the dining room at 6:30 P.M. each night with place settings and the TV off. Her husband agreed to make a special effort for that month to arrive home in time for dinner. At the end of the month, the entire family decided to continue the ritual, as they had enjoyed the sense of connection and stability it provided.

Another client, never an exerciser, worried as midlife had expanded his stomach more and more. He convinced his next-door neighbor to walk for 1 hour with him each night. They both enjoyed the uninterrupted time to walk, get out in nature, and talk with each other.

Creating or Finding Meaning in Suffering or Life

There was a cartoon in the *New Yorker* magazine in which two women were walking down the street. One said to the other, "I wonder what this series of meaningless experiences is trying to tell me."

Someone has suggested that instead of *homo sapiens*, we humans should be called *homo narrans*, or storytelling people. We seem to have a need to make meaning, stories, from our lives, and if this meaning is missing or unsatisfying, we suffer as a result. Sometimes our life stories or meanings get disrupted by trauma or loss, or we may lose the thread of meaning. Helping clients restore or find meaningful stories or interpretations of their lives can give them bigger connections and purpose.

Sometimes I ask my clients who seem drifting or lost: Do you think you are just a random collection of DNA wandering this planet, destined to eat, excrete, and reproduce, or do you think you have a bigger purpose or reason for being alive? This may elicit a statement about meaninglessness or my clients may tell me the larger meaning or purpose they have discovered for their lives. If they don't have such a bigger story or purpose, I suggest that they search in several directions. I am not suggesting that these stories are "the way it is," only that they are a tool that some people use and others might find useful in making sense of difficult times or situations.

Joseph Campbell (1988) made the phrase "follow your bliss" famous. He suggested that if people followed what fascinated them and brought their souls satisfaction, they would find their life's work and life would work out. The word *bliss* is related in its origins to the word *wound*. In French, wound or injury is *blessure*, so I would like to recommend another path to helping clients finding their destinies and life's work: they should follow their wounds.

Patsy Rodenberg, the well-respected vocal coach for actors, was once asked whether or not she ever had vocal problems (Gross, 2004). She replied that of course she had. One couldn't coach other people with sympathy, she asserted, unless one has had difficulties in the same area. She had a stutter as a child and also could not pronounce certain sounds. She was sent to an elocution teacher, who terrified her. She was never able to accomplish what the elocution teacher wanted. She was also mocked by the other children at school. Out of these experiences came her life's work. From her wound came her destiny.

Candy Lightener, whose daughter was killed by a repeat drunk driver, found her life's work by dedicating herself to reducing drunk driving. She founded the organization Mothers Against Drunk Driving (M.A.D.D.), which works to make better laws and ensure they are enforced.

Another parent who lost a child, John Walsh, began hosting a television show whose purpose was to locate criminals with the help of tips from the general public. The show has led to the capture and conviction of a large number of criminals who might have remained at large if not for *America's Most Wanted*. Walsh's son, Adam, was abducted and killed at a young age. John Walsh took that wound and turned it into his crusade to capture criminals and put them behind bars.

One way of making meaning from problems is to turn them into the energy to make a contribution to the world—to use one's pain to lessen the suffering of others.

Questions for clients could include:

- How have you become sensitized to the pain of others through this problem?
- Is there anything you could do to make the world a better place or to reduce the likelihood that others will suffer as you have?

THE BIGGER PICTURE

Finding some larger context or bigger meaning in which to situate the difficulties clients face can help them move on or relieve suffering.

There is an old story about a farmer whose horse is stolen. Neighbors commiserate with him about his loss but he responds with equanimity. "Maybe it's a bad thing, maybe not." They shake their heads in wonder. How could it not be a bad thing? They dismiss him as crazy. When the horse shows up again a few weeks later, obviously not having been stolen but merely having wandered away, those same neighbors congratulate him on his good fortune. Again he demurs. "Perhaps it's good luck, perhaps not." The neighbors are now convinced this fool doesn't know a thing. But when his son is thrown from the horse some days later, they are beginning to see what he means. He needs his son to help with the harvest. Without his son to help, his profits from the crop will be severely diminished. But again the farmer says, "Maybe this broken leg is a tragedy, or it might be a blessing in disguise." And when all the young men are drafted into the army to fight a war, they all realize his wisdom because his son is spared the draft due to his broken leg. And so it goes.

This story shows that there can be a bigger story in life that we don't have access to at the moment. Religious people attribute this bigger story to God. Man makes plans and God laughs, goes the saying. God's ways are a mystery. But regardless of whether or not one attributes the bigger picture to God's plans, there is often some comfort in the idea that there is a bigger story to which we don't have access. The story is not over until life ends.

Questions for clients:

• Do you think your life or this incident is part of some larger meaning that you don't have access to right now?
• How do you think this fits into the bigger picture of your life?

LEADING SOMEWHERE

A variation on the bigger-picture theme is the idea that one's current life, even mistakes and problems, may be necessary precursors that lead toward somewhere else. I heard a country song recently that talked about all the mistakes and heartaches a guy went through, but in the end he blessed the broken road that had led him to his current love.

Some inquiries that might highlight this theme are:

• Can you think of past traumas or problems that actually led you to a better place and that seem necessary experiences when you look back on them?
• Do you think what you are going through right now could be one of those kinds of experiences?

GUIDED BY AN INVISIBLE HAND

This is the idea that there is an invisible hand, that of God or a guardian angel, that is guiding us through this life, protecting us, or leading us somewhere. Again, since we don't have access to the destination or purpose, we must trust the invisible hand.

Questions for clients might include:

- Do you think your life is guided in any way?
- Do you have the sense that you have a guardian angel or another entity that takes an active interest in your life and has an influence over your particular life?
- Have you learned to trust this guiding hand or influence? Or are there times when you trust and times when you doubt or lose faith? If you lose faith, how can you get back to trust?

LESSONS LEARNED

The therapist has to be careful with lessons learned. It could come across as too glib or could sound invalidating of clients' suffering. It involves asking clients to search for lessons learned and wisdom gained from problems.

Possible questions include:

- Without being dismissive of your suffering, I was wondering if you think there was any lesson you have learned from this experience?
- How do you think your life is somehow better because of this problem, even though you wouldn't have chosen it?
- What do you think you could contribute to the world or other people now that you have gone through this difficult time?

A client of mine was feeling very stressed because it seemed like all her friends, co-workers, and family members were having crises all at once. She was spending her time talking on the phone, buying groceries for sick friends, and lending money to others. When I asked her if there was any lesson to be learned from this stress, she immediately brightened up. Instead of talking about the stress, she began to re-conceptualize it as an opportunity to find a balance between taking care of others and taking care of herself. She said she had struggled with this issue for years and now that she was in therapy it was a perfect time to finally work it out. We began to talk about listening to her body, which usually signaled to her that she was doing too much or was too stressed through back pain and burning eyes, and how to politely tell others she wasn't available to help them at the moment.

THE NEXT LIFE WILL BE BETTER

Many clients find solace in this story: The suffering in this life is tolerable or even good because it will lead to a better life in the hereafter or in the next incarnation. This life is merely the prelude to another one, in heaven or paradise or in the clients' next rebirth. Suffering seems to earn one credit in that next life. Or at least it makes the suffering in this life more tolerable.

Questions for clients along these lines include:

• What do you think happens when we die?
• Do you think that if we suffer in this life, we will find relief or reward in the afterlife?

• Do you think people are reborn? If so, what do you make of this experience you are going through right now?

FAITH

Take the first step in faith. You don't have to see the whole staircase, just take the first step.   —DR. MARTIN LUTHER KING, JR.

Often in the midst of problems, things look pretty bad. Sometimes the only way forward is through faith. Having faith means stepping into the unknown with no guarantees that things will work out.

Alan Watts, the former Anglican bishop who became an expert in Asian religions, made a useful distinction between belief and faith. Belief, derived from the old English word *lief* (which means "wish"), refers to the idea that a person wishes that things are the way one thinks. Faith is very different thing, in his view: "Faith . . . is an unreserved opening of the mind to the truth, whatever it may turn out to be. Faith has no preconceptions; it is a plunge into the unknown. Belief clings, but faith lets go . . . faith is the essential virtue of science, and likewise of any religion that is not self-deception" (Johnson, 2003).

A similar distinction is made by former prisoner of war, the late James Stockdale, who maintained that faith is different from optimism. He said that the prisoners who got discouraged were the optimists, who kept believing that they would be released by Christmas. Christmas would come and go. Then the optimists asserted that they would be released by Easter. And Easter would come and go as well. By the time the next Christmas rolled around, they would give up, their optimism defeated by reality. "This is a very important lesson," said Stockdale. "You must never confuse faith that you will prevail in the end—which you can never afford to lose—with the need for discipline to confront the most brutal facts of your current reality, whatever they might be" (in Collins, 2001).

In one of my workshops, a Jewish scholar told me that most people get their image of the Israelites crossing the Red Sea from the movies. According to Jewish scholars, what actually happened was a little different from the movie version. The Israelites, being pursued by the Egyptians, prayed to God. God said, in effect, "Sure, I'll help you. But you have to show me you have faith first by plunging into the water with the possibility you could drown." The first one to comply was Nachshon. He went into the water to his nose to show he trusted God. Then God parted the waters.

Indiana Jones and Kierkegaard are my models for faith. There is a scene in an Indiana Jones movie in which he must step out into a deep chasm. He has been told that he must step out in faith, but it seems a crazy thing to do. He must step out without assurances and evidence. Finally he takes the plunge and finds that, instead of falling to his death, there is a hidden bridge that holds him.

The difference between Indy and Kierkegaard? Kierkegaard said that by stepping out in good faith, we create the bridge to the next place in our lives.

Sometimes our clients have to be encouraged to step out in faith. "I'll never find another relationship!" cries the client. "No one will ever love me. I'm a mess." I send such clients to the shopping mall sometimes, to observe all the people that have relationships. Some of them are not the most attractive people in the world or don't seem like they have it together, but still they have partners. Of course, there is the possibility that clients will never find a relationship, but that is made more likely if they become withdrawn and act as if it will be the case. Here is a quotation from one of my definitive spiritual resources, the *USA Today* newspaper.

> Faith is the ability to look at the world we have created and see possibility, even as we acknowledge our capacity for destruction. It is the glue that holds our fractured pieces together and allows us to continue beyond all reason. The faith we seek is not the comfort of having all the answers. Rather, it is the will to keep asking the questions. Faith is the voice in the night that says we will go on (Whitney, 1999).

I sometimes suggest that my clients write themselves a letter from the future, after things have worked out or they have moved on, as a way of eliciting and connecting with faith.

Here are instructions I typically give clients:

1. Write a letter from your future self to your current self from five years from now.

2. Describe where you are, what you are doing, and what you have gone through to get there.
3. Tell yourself the crucial things you realized or did to get there.
4. Give yourself some sage and compassionate advice from the future.

Here are some questions you might ask your clients about faith:

- When have you taken a scary step and yet trusted that things would work out?
- Where do you need to take such a step right now?
- What is the time in your life when you have most relied on or needed faith?

Several books are helpful to suggest to clients regarding faith, hope, and meaning. A classic many people have found comforting and inspirational is Viktor Frankl's (1997) *Man's Search for Meaning*. Another title that many clients have found helpful is Rabbi Harold Kushner's (1981) *When Bad Things Happen to Good People*.

The Two Functions of the Soul

I often see people in therapy who seem disconnected from their souls. They don't seem to have a sense of why they are on the planet or they seem lacking in energy and integrity. Sometimes therapists help clients to identify their soul signals and reconnect to their deepest selves by tapping into the two functions of the soul.

The first function of the soul is that it seems to want to integrate disparate aspects of our personalities. The logical mind wants to figure out whether we are kind or selfish, afraid or confident, crazy or sane. The soul has no such push. The soul seems to have room for contradictions within us and wants to contain them in the same space.

Not only does the soul have room for these seeming contradictions, but there seems to be a longing for integration. If we disregard or neglect or try to suppress aspects of ourselves for too long, the soul calls us to bring them back to our lives.

Here are some questions therapists can pose to clients that can illuminate issues surrounding integrity and integration for clients:

- Where do you feel like a fake, an imposter, lying, faking, hiding who you are, divided against yourself?
- What are some of the ways in which you have opposite feelings or personality aspects?
- What are some of the contradictions with which you live?
- What is one step you could take toward embracing or including those polarities, opposites, or contradictions?
- What permission(s) might you need to help you include or allow these opposites?
- How do you know when something you are doing or planning does not have integrity for you?
- What has helped you integrate more of who you are into your life?

• Who are your role models for integrity and integration? What are they like and how would you or could you be more like they are in the areas of integrity and integration?

The second soul function is an energizing one. We lose our souls when we lose our unique and vital energy, which we sometimes do when we lose hope or when we give up too much of our own sensibilities to fit in or be loved.

I have identified two main sources of energy: what we love and what we don't like. Either one can energize us. That is, we can derive energy and motivation from being in bliss or from being upset. For shorthand, I call these two energies Blissed and Pissed (sorry for the informality, but, hey, they do rhyme and are easy to remember and they do make the point).

Blissed refers to the things we are passionate about in a positive way. These are the things that we love and make us deeply happy.

Pissed refers to the things in this world that upset us enough to be moved to try to correct them. This is as much a source of energy in many lives as the happy, positive energy is.

Here are some questions therapists can use to determine what energizes or animates clients:

• In what areas of your life is your energy high?
• In what areas of your life is your energy low?

- In what areas of your life is the energy mixed? What makes the difference?
- What drains or diminishes your energy?
- What increases your energy?
- What are the things, situations, or people that energize you, make you feel alive, and cause your heart to sing?
- What situations or circumstances that upset you do you have the energy to do something about.
- Remember a time when you had energy and aliveness. What did it feel like in your body? What kinds of thoughts would you think? How did you move?
- What do you do that takes effort, but you seek it out anytime you get some time? It could be hiking in the mountains, painting a picture, writing, spending time with your children, working, or other things.
- Who are your role models for aliveness and passion? What are they like and how would you or could you be more like they are in the areas of aliveness and passion?

CHAPTER TWO

Pathways
to Compassion

❋

This is my simple religion. There is no need for temples;
no need for complicated philosophy. Our own brain, our own
heart is our temple; the philosophy is kindness.
—DALAI LAMA

HERE I WILL PRESENT a developmental model that I
have presented elsewhere (O'Hanlon, 2003) that is a cor-
nerstone of the approach to compassion to which I adhere.

In my view, the process of socialization begins to divide
us from ourselves as we learn from our families, our gender training, and our peers that certain aspects of our personal experience and our nature are unacceptable or
shameful. I call these split-off feelings "missing pieces." "Big
boys don't cry," males soon learn. "Don't be a girl." "You're
such a sissy." Girls learn to be soft-spoken, to keep their
knees together, to be ladylike, to be sensitive to others'
needs and take care of others before they care for them-

selves, and so on. In the case of a family in which a child died in stillbirth, all talk of this lost child, or of death, grief, and loss in general, may have been implicitly forbidden. This memory and the feelings of grief become the missing pieces, banned from one's experience as unacceptable.

At other times these missing pieces result from the process of acculturation. For example, on my visits to Australia and England, I noticed that there was an unwritten rule: Don't put yourself forward or stand out from the crowd. (Americans, typically, have no such restraint.)

Still other distorting effects come through trauma, when some aspects of our physical or sensory experience become separated from our sense of ourselves. We dissociate from our sexuality, our sense memories, parts of our bodies, or other aspects during the trauma, since we are so overwhelmed with shame or flooded by painful or shameful feelings. This is a natural and understandable response to trauma, but sometimes it becomes a habit when it is no longer necessary for survival or coping.

I have referred to this process as the 3-D process: Dissociate, Disown, and Devalue. We not only separate from the experience, we shift it out of our sense of identity, and we somehow decide that the aspect is bad, shameful, or invalid.

The unfortunate effect of this process is that this un-integrated aspect develops a life of its own, seemingly operating beyond our will and control (see Figure 2.1). Two things often happen as a result (I call these two effects *inhibition* and *intrusion*). One is that our access to this expe-

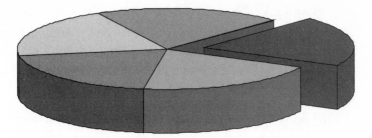

FIGURE 2.1. THE 3-D PROCESS: SPLIT-OFF ASPECTS BECOME
UNINTEGRATED AND DEVELOP A LIFE OF THEIR OWN.

rience diminishes; that is, we feel numb in this area. We
can't remember some part of our childhood or earlier life;
we can't cry; or we feel no joy (*inhibition*). The other effect
is that we occasionally feel overwhelmed or intruded upon
by this unowned aspect. We can't forget our past as it in-
trudes as flashbacks. Or we develop automatic and com-
pulsive behavior. We act out sexually, having affairs or
surfing the Internet for hours for pornographic sites (*intrusion*). Poet David Whyte wrote: "There seems to be
some connection between the places we have disowned
inside ourselves and the key to where we need to go. Life
as usual has arranged a way in which we're not allowed
to leave anything behind that is not somehow resolved"
(Whyte, 1995). And another poet, Robert Frost, wrote:
"Something we were withholding made us weak until we
found it was ourselves" (Executive Speaker, 2005).

Indeed, the structure of bigotry, racism, and ethnic/na-
tionalistic violence is similar to the process of exclusion

and devaluing in the inner world. The bad stuff is projected on the "other" and energy is expended to keep the "other" contained, or even in killing off the bad "others" (as in ethnic cleansing in the former Yugoslavia; in Uganda; in Sudan; and in Nazi Germany).

What is the spiritually based help for this exclusion and devaluing? It has two elements: inclusion and compassion.

According to Transactional Analysis (TA), some part of our lives is run by injunctions—unconscious restraints or compulsions that reside in our deep beliefs about ourselves and our lives. *You must succeed. You can never make mistakes. You must get along with everyone. You should be nice. You have to run over others to get ahead.* And so on. These injunctions have two forms: (a) what one must do or be (compelling injunctions); and (b) what one shouldn't or must not or can't do or be.

Challenging these old injunctions takes a rather simple form: giving one of two kinds of permission. The first is *permission to*. This involves somehow communicating to clients that they are okay if they have certain experiences or feelings. "It's okay to feel afraid," the therapist might offer to a client for whom this has been forbidden. "You can make mistakes," might be helpful for a client driven by perfectionism. "It's okay to remember" or "It's okay to forget" might be helpful for a client who has dissociated childhood traumatic memories.

The second kind of permission is *permission not to have to*. "You don't have to be perfect." Or "It's okay not to please others all the time." Or "You don't have to remember everything in order to move on."

There are many ways to get this permission across: merely giving verbal permission; giving task assignments (go out and make five mistakes this week); doing psychodrama (have someone play the part of the client who acts out sexually and someone else play the part of the client who acts sexually appropriate); cognitive challenges to the irrational nature of these beliefs; and so on. The point of whatever intervention the therapist uses is that it must touch the client experientially—it won't do to be merely a good idea that the client agrees makes sense rationally. These split-off parts live in a more irrational and experiential place within the client, so just telling the client the ideas probably won't move him or her.

There is a more complex form of inclusion that involves bringing together disparate, seemingly opposite aspects within the client so that the aspects can coexist. We have phrases in the English language that illustrate these polarities coexisting:

That was *terribly kind* of you.
Parting is such *sweet sorrow*.
I went on a *working vacation*.

My former mentor and teacher, Milton Erickson, used to use expressions like these in his hypnosis and therapy. He maintained that if the therapist didn't speak both sides of the patient's ambivalence, the patient would be compelled to act out the unspoken or unacknowledged side. "If you don't say the 'no,' the patient will," he used to intone.

Here are a few memorable examples of his use of such methods of inclusion:

"You really *want* to change, do you *not?*"
"It's important to *remember* to *forget* and *forget* to *remember.*"
"You can be *elaborately casual* in the way you wash your hands compulsively."

In a spiritually based therapy, these phrases and similar processes are used to include aspects of the client that the rational process, based in Aristotelian logic of either-or thinking, may leave out. We are either lazy or diligent, our rational minds tell us. But the truth may be that we are both diligent and lazy; both careful and sloppy. We can be protected and vulnerable at the same time, anxious and calm.

Poets and artists seem to get this better than most. Poet Donald Hall wrote: "In logic, no two things can occupy the same point at the same time, and in poetry that happens all the time. This is almost what poetry is for, to be able to embody contrary feelings in the same motion." And poet Walt Whitman said it this way: "Do I contradict myself? Very well, then I contradict myself. I am large, I contain multitudes" (Whitman, 2001).

Helping clients accept and value these inner contradictions can help the process of inclusion of the excluded aspects of themselves, their "missing pieces."

Here are some questions and queries regarding inclusion that therapists might use with clients:

- What aspect of you have you had trouble coming to terms with?
- If you were to name the two most contradictory aspects of your personality, what would they be?
- Tell me something about a time when you experienced opposite feelings at the same time.

Table 2.1 on the following page summarizes what we have covered in the section above.

DEVELOPING COMPASSION

Related to this inclusive approach is compassion: compassion for oneself and compassion toward others.

Compassion involves softening toward oneself and toward others. Its opposites are judgments and harshness toward oneself and/or others. When we think others are bad or we judge them or their intentions harshly, we are not feeling compassion. The etymological roots of compassion point to this sense as well. Its roots are *passion* (to feel) and *com* (with). So compassion means to feel with, and not against, oneself or others.

THE PROBLEM: INJUNCTIONS

Determine the injunctions that may have dominated your clients. These are conclusions that the clients have made about themselves or ideas that other people have suggested to them or told them are true. They can usually be thought of in two forms:

1. Have to/should/must (as in "You must always be perfect" or "I have to hurt myself") or
2. Can't/shouldn't/don't (as in "You shouldn't feel sexual feelings" or "I can't be angry").

SELF-DEVALUING

Sometimes clients have come to the conclusion, consciously or unconsciously, that they are bad or that parts of them are bad. They might say, "If you only knew what I am like inside, you would see that I am evil." They might have the sense that anger is bad and they shouldn't feel it or show it. If they do feel it or show it, they think they are are very bad or that anger is very bad.

THE SOLUTION: VALUING, PERMISSION, AND INCLUSION AS ANTIDOTES

1. Give clients permission to and permission not to have to experience or be something. For example, "You can feel angry and you don't have to feel angry." Or "It's okay to be sexual and you don't have to be sexual." Be careful when giving permission about actions.
2. Suggest the possibility of having seeming opposites or contradictions coexist without conflict. For example, "You can tell me and not tell me about the abuse."

TABLE 2.1. SUMMARY OF INCLUSION AND PERMISSION.

Self-Compassion

After 30-plus years as a therapist, I have been amazed to realize that most of the clients I have seen in therapy think there is something fundamentally unacceptable or unworthy about themselves. This seems to be a wide-spread condition. Perhaps we all carry around an image of what it is to be a good person, a good husband, an attractive woman, a successful person. And we rarely match up to these images and expectations.

Self-compassion helps people accept themselves as they are. *Lord, help me accept the truth about myself no matter how good it is*, is a saying someone passed on to me recently. In part, this involves accepting that we are human and therefore not perfect. In part, this involves caring for ourselves as we are. When my clients criticize themselves, I sometimes ask them to imagine that their best friends or children have the traits and self-criticisms. How would the clients reassure them that they were okay or acceptable?

Often this nonacceptance comes in the area of the body. There has been much discussion on the pressure our society and the media put on females to have a certain kind of body type and the relationship of this pressure to the prevalence of eating disorders. But it seems to me that males are now experiencing a similar kind of pressure and self-criticalness.

One of my models in the area of self-compassion was the late psychiatrist and family therapist Carl Whitaker (2001). It is said that near the end of his life, Whitaker met up with one of his longtime critics, a man who had judged him harshly and made his criticisms of Whitaker quite public. On their first encounter in many years, Whitaker smiled wistfully at his longtime nemesis and said, "If it's any consolation to you, I've been a great disappointment to myself in this life as well." Therapists can help clients accept their failings, their humanness.

Here are some questions therapists can pose to help evoke self-compassion in clients:

- Is there any area in which you are critical or non-accepting of yourself?
- What do you think is your most unacceptable aspect or part of your body?
- What is one step you could take toward valuing or at least moving toward accepting that aspect?
- If that trait or aspect were one of your best friend's, how would you assure him or her it is okay?

Compassion Toward Others

One way to develop compassion toward others is to find something of yourself in them. Carl Jung said: "Everything that irritates us about others can lead us to an understanding of ourselves" (1955). Imago relationship therapy posits that whatever irritates us about others is usually the result of neglected, projected aspects of ourselves or unfinished issues we have with our parents from our early years. In his novel *Underworld*, Don DeLillo wrote: "It's not enough to hate your enemy. You have to understand how the two of you bring each other to a deep completion" (1998).

Even if this psychological proposition is not true, clients can find ways to be more compassionate to others by accepting them as the flawed and imperfect humans they are. Lloyd Shearer advised: "Resolve to be tender with the young, compassionate with the aged, sympathetic with the striving, and tolerant with the weak and the wrong. Sometime in life you will have been all of these."

Here are some areas to examine and questions for therapists to ask their clients regarding compassion toward others:

- Can you imagine that whatever you find yourself judging harshly about others is actually something you have not accepted about yourself? How could you begin to accept that aspect of yourself if this were true?
- Does your life create an atmosphere of compassion, rather than judgement or harshness? How could you create or enhance an atmosphere of compassion and kindness?
- If this person (or you) were your child or best friend, how would you view or relate to him or her?
- Think of the most serene, compassionate, or wise person or figure you know. How would he or she view this situation or deal with it?
- Remember a time when you were judgmental or critical of someone and then softened or were more com-

passionate. How did you make that shift? What changed after you made that shift? Can you apply any of that to your current situation?

Compassion played an important role in a case I once worked on, helping a couple with marital trouble. In one session, the wife reported that she was very upset because she had talked to the husband's niece and nephew, and they had told her how sorry they were that she was getting a divorce. She told them she was not getting a divorce, but that their uncle and she were merely having some problems and that they were trying to work them out. The niece and nephew seemed surprised and told her that her husband had told them on a visit just the day before that he had filed for divorce. When she talked to her husband, he confirmed that it was true. In a moment of anger, he had filed papers. He had withdrawn them when they began getting along a bit better the next day and decided not to mention it to her. She was hurt by the fact that he told his nephew and niece but not her; she was also hurt by the fact that he had filed at all. The husband responded rather coldly that she should just drop the matter, since he hadn't gone through with it. This dismissal upset her further.

In exploring the matter, our discussion led back to a moment from the husband's past in which his father had walked out on his mother, while he, as a nine-year-old boy, had stood on the front steps and cried out of fear and grief. As he described that moment, the husband, usually very cold and rational, began to sob. His wife was moved to witness this and took his hand to comfort him. After that session, every time he got cold and distant, she told me she would remember that, at that moment, he was really a scared and hurt little boy. This evocation of compassion went a long way toward healing the rift between them.

FORGIVENESS

Related to compassion is the notion of forgiveness. Some interesting work has been done in various countries around the world on reconciliation and forgiveness, most famously by the South African Truth and Reconciliation Commission. While this work was more on a social level than a therapeutic one, it is worth mentioning here to give some beginning guidelines for using forgiveness in therapy. The ground rules of the Truth and Reconciliation Commission were simple: People who had committed atrocities during the time of apartheid could come before the commission; if they told the truth, they would be given an amnesty from prosecution. (There were some legal exceptions to this rule that were clear to the participants.) If the perpetrators did not come forward or if they lied during the proceedings or left out substantial things they had done, they would be prosecuted. Something similar seems to help in more individual situations of injury and forgiveness.

Many victims of wrongdoing often desperately want facts about what really happened and an explanation of how the perpetrators justified their actions. Women whose husbands were tortured and murdered by one of the most notorious white South African officials had never heard what happened to their missing spouses. Hearing their torture and murders described at least gave them closure. And the fact that the perpetrator cried while telling them the story and told them he was terribly sorry for what he had done made him appear more human than monster to them. Some of the women offered him forgiveness after this meeting.

Of course, it usually helps if the perpetrator offers an admission of wrongdoing, not just a recitation of facts. And offering apologies and amends, if appropriate, can help foster the forgiveness process.

I mention this example to make some distinctions that will be helpful in applying this process in therapy. Forgiveness does not mean letting the perpetrator off the hook and not holding him or her accountable when they have done one wrong. It does not mean forgetting what happened. Forgiveness asks something from the perpetrator as well as the victim.

One motivation of victims to forgive those who have done them wrong may be to obtain relief from bitterness and stress. A study found that people who are unable to forgive themselves or others also have an increased incidence of depression and callousness toward others

(Pargament et al., 1998). Other studies or reviews have noted that the act of forgiveness seems to reduce depression and anxiety; the act of forgiveness leads to better coping with stress, increased closeness to others, and an increase in physical well-being (Witvliet, Ludwig & VanderLaan, 2001; Worthington, 1998).

A woman whose daughter had been killed in a street crime was unable to move on with her life. She came to therapy and part of the discussion involved a project that I had seen on *Oprah*. It involved victims or relatives of victims visiting their perpetrators in prison, with some clear guidelines for discussion, in order to find some measure of peace. At first, my client said that this wasn't for her, but several weeks later, after discussions with friends and some investigation of the process on the Internet, she decided to pursue it. The discussion she had with her daughter's killer was somewhat helpful and somewhat frustrating (he blamed the murder on his bad upbringing), but it helped her begin to see the murderer as another human being rather than as a monster. There was other therapeutic work to do, but the small measure of forgiveness she found in that visit was a piece of her healing.

The process of forgiveness suggested for the perpetrator, then, is:

1. Acknowledge the wrong or hurt done. Tell the truth about what you have done.

2. Take responsibility. Don't blame others or factors beyond your control. This doesn't mean you can't explain mitigating circumstances and good intentions gone awry, just that you be very careful that such explanations do not appear to excuse you from accountability in the matter. You made choices and did things that caused harm.

3. Offer an apology if appropriate.

4. Offer to make amends, to the person or to society, if appropriate. This may involve some sort of sacrifice or repentance or reparations.

5. Make a commitment not to repeat the harmful behavior in the future. This does not mean that the person or people harmed must believe or accept this pledge. It might take time to reestablish trust, which may, ultimately, never be restored.

6. Ask for forgiveness, again, if appropriate. This should not be done before the other steps and, again, it may not be granted. Care should be taken not to ask this forgiveness too quickly or too lightly.

The process of forgiveness for the wronged person might involve the following steps:

1. Confront the wrongdoer, in person, in writing, or through a third party to mediate and facilitate.

2. Ask for a truthful account and an explanation. Be careful not to allow their explanation to let them off the hook for what he or she has done.

3. Ask for an apology or amends, if appropriate or acceptable. This is always up to the wronged one. If it would feel like a new hurt to hear this from the perpetrator, do not seek it, obviously.

4. Let go of bitterness, desire for revenge or retaliation, and resentment. No one can tell you that you have to do this, but there is evidence that carrying this bitterness, resentment, and desire for retaliation or revenge is harmful to you.

5. Use this hurt to energize a positive contribution you could make to the world or to understand how you were vulnerable to this kind of hurt so you can be more likely to avoid being in such a situation in the future, if possible.

6. If the relationship with the offender is going to continue, ask for more caring or trustworthy behavior from him or her in the future.

7. If the offender continues to hurt you, take steps to protect yourself and provide consequences that make it likely that the offender will be motivated to stop hurting you.

In the Christian Bible, Christ told his followers that if they forgave others, he would forgive them. How many times are they expected to forgive? Seventy times 7, he admonishes them. Other religions also stress the importance of compassion and forgiveness. The Dalai Lama gave a talk in which he discussed Tibetan Buddhism as well as the devastation the Chinese had done to his country and culture. Some in the audience were angry at the Chinese and tried to get the Dalai Lama to admit that he resented the Chinese for these atrocities, but he refused. Finally, after being pressed many times on this matter, he smiled and said that in Tibetan Buddhism, there is the belief that if one misbehaves in this life, one will suffer for it in future incarnations. Therefore, he spends the first part of his morning meditation each day praying for the Chinese to reduce the suffering they are likely to experience in their next lives. This kind of forgiveness and compassion is central to his religion and he seems to live it completely.

The use of rituals that symbolize leaving the hurt or trauma behind seem to help the process of forgiveness. These rituals can help make real the emotional transition from the trauma to moving on by giving some physicality to the process, providing actions and physical objects to make the inside feelings and sensibilities external and observable.

As a therapist, after ascertaining that the client who has been wronged or hurt is ready to let go of the trauma or injury, help the client find or create an object that symbolizes the injurious situation or hurt emotion. Then have the client take some action with that object that symbolizes letting it go.

I was treating Ben and Sarah in couples therapy. Ben had found out that Sarah had been having an affair. They reconciled after Sarah agreed to give up the affair, but after a few months, Sarah confessed to Ben that she was still in love with the man with whom she had had the affair and was thinking of leaving the marriage. They went to couples counseling, where they decided to separate and divorce after that process made it clear to both of them that the marriage was over.

They met one day at a shared storage unit, and were dividing their possessions when they came across a polished stone heart that Ben had given Sarah during their courtship. While in storage, the heart had broken in two. Ben and Sarah silently looked at each other after the box was opened. Then Ben took the heart with him. Some time later, when he had done the grieving he needed to do and was ready to let the relationship go, he went to the forest where he and Sarah had often walked together and buried that broken heart by the footpath. That physical action—a ritual—of letting go helped Ben begin to move to compassion for Sarah as he let go of his bitterness.

WITNESSING AND DEEP EMPATHY DURING SUFFERING

Sometimes, when our clients are suffering, the most spiritual help we can give them is just to be a compassionate witness to their suffering. Those who work in hospice know that sometimes there is not a problem to be solved, but merely suffering and loss to be lived. This is true in situations other than death and dying. Not all problems brought to therapists have solutions. We might try our best to help people resolve problems, but it doesn't always work.

I saw a movie some years ago called *What Dreams May Come*. One of the characters in the movie (played by Annabella Sciorra) kills herself and goes to hell. Her beloved husband (played by Robin Williams) has also died and gone to heaven. He determines that he will rescue her from hell, but is told by the angels that this is impossible. He won't accept this and begins a journey to find and retrieve her. But when he arrives in hell, she does not recognize him and begins to run away in fear. He has been told that the only way to find her and reconnect is to bring forth shared memories, so he begins to tell her a story of their lives together. They had lost their children in a tragic accident and she had tried to kill herself at that time because she blamed herself for their deaths (she was supposed to pick them up from school but work interfered and they died in a car accident on the way home from school that day). Robin Williams's character had been visiting his wife in the psychiatric hospital to which she was committed after the suicide attempt. He had been trying to convince her that she was not to blame for their children's deaths and that she should rejoin him in life. She stopped responding to these entreaties and began to turn away from him when he visited.

One day he arrived at the hospital and told her he finally understood what the problem had been. He had thought she had turned from him because he reminded her of the lost children, but now he realized that the real problem was that he had left her alone in her pain. He had not been able to accept her view that she was to blame for the children's deaths and had resisted this view. He now realized that she was right and he hadn't understood. "What's true in our minds is true." For the first time, she turned toward him, held him close, and began to cry. She returned to life with him after he joined her in her pain and self-recrimination.

I experienced a similar understanding of empathy when my wife became seriously ill and discouraged about her chances of recovery. Any time she spoke about giving up, I would respond with some positive frame of reference (i.e., this is just a temporary setback; it isn't so bad; we will find a new treatment that will surely work; and so on). We watched *What Dreams May Come Together* and had a discussion about it afterwards. "That is what I feel like when you get so positive when I am so discouraged," she told me, "I feel left alone." The next time the situation occurred, I bit my tongue and listened. Instead of offering positive possibilities, I asked questions about her discouragement.

In another example of the importance of cultivating empathy *and* compassion, rather than just blanket encouragement or good wishes, a character in Harlan Coben's novel *Tell No One* (Coben, 2001) reports the ill effects of people trying to comfort him after his wife's death:

> Well-meaning friends . . . handed me the usual clichés, and so I feel in a pretty good position to warn you: Just offer your deepest condolences. Don't tell me I'm young. Don't tell me it'll get better. Don't tell me she's in a better place. Don't tell me that it's part of some divine plan. Don't tell me that I was lucky to have had such a love. Every one of these platitudes pissed me off.

Not long after my experience with my wife's illness, I was counseling a couple and the wife complained that she was responsible for everything in their family and around the house. The husband reacted strongly. He had flexible hours in his job, he told me, and was almost always the one who took the children to medical appointments, picked them up at school when they became ill, and met the workmen at the house when home repairs were needed. He also cooked for the family twice a week.

Even after his passionate case, his wife remained adamant that she was responsible for everything. Instead of reacting like he did, I told her to explain what she meant by "responsible." She said that while her husband did a lot of the household and family tasks, she was the one who had to remember that the tasks were to be done or scheduled. She remembered that the children needed a dental or medical checkup. She noticed the leaking shower and called the plumber. She bought the groceries and planned the meals. If they were both busy, it was assumed that she would worry about and arrange childcare. She said she felt exhausted from worrying about everything and being responsible for things. At first, her husband still did not understand the difference between doing things and feeling responsible for them. But I asked him to listen more deeply as she explained it again. Finally, he got beyond his defensive reaction.

In yet another example of the benefits of being a compassionate listener, I once came across an interview with a psychologist who specialized in treating sexually violent criminals. She had a chance to interview Jeffrey Dahmer, a serial killer who tortured and ate his victims. He told her that fantasies of killing animals had begun for him in his teens, but he resisted these fantasies and tried to stop them. He never told anybody about them and they grew in intensity until he could no longer contain them and he began to act them out. This psychologist said that she was treating a teenager with similar fantasies and the fantasies had begun to diminish in intensity because he verbalized them to her in therapy. The teenage client found that he was not condemned. What a different outcome these two situations had! In one, a compassionate listener was available; in the other, the person was left with shame and a growing sense of compulsion.

Viktor Frankl (2000) tells the story of a woman who, having read Frankl's books, called him out of the blue one night at 3 A.M., telling him she intended to end her life. Frankl listened respectfully to her reasons for suicide and gave her his best argument for staying alive. She was not convinced, but agreed to come to see him at his office at 9 A.M. that morning. When she arrived, she informed him that none of his arguments had moved her to stay alive, but what had was that she had called him in the middle of the night and he was patient with her. Not only that, he had agreed, after an interrupted night's sleep, to meet with her early in the morning. She decided that if there were such kind people in the world, perhaps life was worth living.

Simone Weil, who dedicated her life to relieving suffering, said, "The capacity to give one's attention to a sufferer is a very rare and difficult thing; it is almost a miracle; it is a miracle" (1991).

I saw a family in therapy once that stymied me. I am a pretty optimistic person, but after about five meetings with this family, I found myself getting very discouraged. Each week they appeared with a new major problem: one week two of the children had broken into their middle school and caused $40,000 worth of damage. They were caught and the parents had to pay the cost. They next week, that trouble seemed to be forgotten as they told me about the father accidentally running over one of the children as he backed the car out of the driveway (miraculously, the child escaped any serious or permanent harm). The next week, they never mentioned the school damage or the car. One of the children had taken a bite— literally a chunk of fur and skin—from the family dog in retaliation for the dog having bitten him. After those first five sessions, I confessed one night to the family that I did not think I was helping them and wondered why they kept coming to see me. They seemed surprised by this and told me that they had seen many other therapists over the years and I was the only one that had never gotten angry with them. I almost cried when I heard that. They were hungry for someone to listen empathically and sympathetically.

One of the ways we don't listen is to oversimplify or generalize people's feelings or situations. I was watching an interview with a woman with a serious degenerative disease who was fighting for the legal right to end her own life. She was being interviewed by a television interviewer. "Why do you want to kill yourself?" the interviewer asked.

"I don't actually want to kill myself. I love life," she answered. "I just don't want to live like this. I can't do anything for myself. There's no freedom and no dignity in it."

"So you want to die?"

"Yes. And I want to live."

The interviewer was confused and couldn't quite grasp the complexity of the situation. The woman wanted to live and she wanted to die. And she wanted the freedom to make her own determination in the matter.

I call this kind of listening in which you are merely with a person who is suffering Deep Listening. (I have been influenced in this area by Arthur Frank [1998] and Arthur Kleinman [1988], both of whom have written very well about the process of catastrophic illness, suffering, and listening to patients' stories.) Deep Listening lets people tell their stories, as confusing, irrational, complicated, or hopeless as they may be.

Guidelines for Deep Listening are:

- Attend to your clients' stories and experiences rather than your idea of the truth or what you think your clients should experience or do. Be willing to do nothing, just be with, acknowledge, and honor your clients' pain and suffering. Just having told their stories can often be powerfully therapeutic.
- Drop, initially at least, the need to change your clients or solve their problem.
- Sit with the clients' pain and suffering with compassion instead of offering positive stories or trying to fix, give advice, or offer suggestions.
- Be aware of the bias you may have toward redemptive stories, stories that lead somewhere positive or have happy endings. Do not try to change, rewrite, reframe, or invalidate the client's nonredemptive, nonhappy story endings.
- Without being patronizing, give credit for small or large efforts or coping and the clients' endurance or strength in facing challenges.
- Avoid platitudes such as "Everything will work out," "God doesn't give you more than you can handle," or "It's going to be all right."

- Avoid glib explanations such as "Why did you create this?," "I wonder what you are meant to learn from this?," or "What part of you needs or benefits from this pain?"
- Speak to the complexity of the situation, including seeming contradictions: "You can't go on suffering like this and you don't want to die," or "You want to give up and you don't want to give up."

Therapists who work in hospice often tell me that one of the reasons for hospice is that relatives and friends keep up a brave face or don't want to listen to discouraged talk or talk about dying.

I once had a client who came to me for a particular therapeutic issue, but in the course of talking to her, I discovered that she had a very discouraging belief. She believed that the world was divided into two kinds of people, the blessed and the cursed. Blessed people could have bad things happen in their lives, but in the end things worked out for them. Cursed people could have good things happen in life, but in the end, and even after death, they were damned and cursed for eternity. Now, she had never asked me to help her change this belief and had just mentioned it in an offhand way one session, but it stuck in my craw. Every session, I would try to get her to change this belief. She very calmly told me that it wasn't a belief, but reality. I was just too cheerful a person to be able to accept this. I found her position maddening and became more subtle in my attempts to dissuade her from this belief, using stories and indirect suggestion. Still, she didn't budge and seemed frustrated with my attempts to change her in this area. Finally, one day, I realized that this was my issue: I couldn't accept that this was the way of the world and I couldn't accept this belief in her. After this realization, I let it go. When I informed her of this, she said, "Good. Now we can focus on what I came to you for and stop wasting energy on that."

Perhaps you as a therapist have some taboo topics, beliefs, or feelings that you try to resist in your clients. Perhaps you are going through some personal crisis and you gently or unconsciously steer your clients away from discussions about the area in which you are having trouble or are in pain. Here are some questions to help you acknowledge any issues in this area that may be interfering with your ability to listen and be with people:

- What discouraging belief or sensibility of your clients have you not been able to accept?
- Are there any feelings of your clients that you find hard to tolerate?
- Where have you been trying to change clients' feelings or attitudes when it might be better to just listen sympathetically?

Akin to being a witness and a presence for people in their suffering is the process of mindfulness, also called self-witnessing. Eastern spiritual traditions developed this process into an art through meditative techniques, but it can be used without knowing or practicing meditation. People have the ability to merely observe their experience, including their suffering, their impulses, their feelings, their thoughts, and their responses, without having to react to or do anything about those experiences. Just noticing and staying with an experience may allow the person to dissolve or move through the experience, or it may give the person time to make different and better choices about how to respond.

Mindfulness, like many other skills, can become easier to use and more powerful with practice. Here is a simple way to use mindfulness in therapy.

1. Identify a place in your clients' lives when they are typically reactive in a way that doesn't serve them or others.
2. Discuss with clients how they can use mindfulness (just noticing rather than doing anything) in that situation.
3. Have them practice mindfulness in that situation and report back on how it worked.

A client of mine had a mother who drove her crazy. Her mother would bail my client out when she got in financial straits, but would also accompany the bailout with a guilt-inducing lecture. I asked her what the typical lecture consisted of. She said she almost had it memorized: "Why aren't you more responsible? You know your stepfather is going to give me grief about bailing you out again and we will get into a huge fight when I get home. Why do you put me in such a situation?" I suggested that, until she became more financially solvent and took care of herself, the lecture was sure to arrive with the money, so why didn't she use it as an opportunity to develop herself spiritually? I explained mindfulness to my client and asked her to pay attention to her own reaction and to pretend that she was the director of a play in which her mother had a role. Every time her mother delivered one of her classic lines, she was to notice how perfect the delivery was. She tried it out during their next similar interaction and found herself smiling during what had previously been so stressful and upsetting. Her mother noticed the different reaction and stopped, saying, "I've said this all before and you've heard it all before, haven't you?" My client replied, "Yes, Mom, but it's okay. I know you need to say these things." They ended up having a better time of it because they didn't get into their usual argument.

In summary, sometimes the most spiritual thing we can do with clients who are suffering is to stay connected to them, not give up, and to be a caring, compassionate, human listener and presence. Sometimes we can coach them to serve the same function for themselves. Sometimes that is enough.

CHAPTER THREE

Pathways
to Contribution

Life's most persistent and urgent question is:
What are you doing for others?
—DR. MARTIN LUTHER KING, JR.

CONTRIBUTION USUALLY COMES out of the first two Cs. When we feel connected to something beyond ourselves and when we feel connected to something more within and beyond ourselves, we are usually moved to make a contribution to others and to the world and to be of service. In his play *Man and Superman*, George Bernard Shaw (2001) holds forth on contribution:

> This is the true joy in life, the being used up for a purpose recognized by yourself as a mighty one; the being a force of nature instead of a feverish, selfish little clod of ailments and grievances, complaining that the world will not devote itself to making you happy.

Gandhi famously said: The best way to find yourself is to lose yourself in the service of others.

There is some research evidence that shows that being of service to others can help oneself. This is often referred to as "doing well by doing good." A University of Michigan study (Brown, 2003) found that couples who reported helping someone else (even as little as once a year) were between 40 and 60% less likely to die than those who reported not helping anyone else during the previous year.

A client of mine had recovered from a severe alcohol problem. During the years he had been drinking, he had often driven drunk. After his recovery, he felt guilty about various things he had done, including driving drunk, and he couldn't seem to resolve the guilt. I spoke to him about the idea of engaging in some kind of reparation. He investigated and discovered a class that was held once a month as a diversion program for people who had been convicted of their first drunk driving offense. He became a regular speaker at the program and people often told him after the program that his was the most effective speech because he had "been there," and wasn't merely a professional lecturing them on why they shouldn't drink and drive. Hearing this, he experienced significant relief from his guilt.

Another client of mine, having seen a bumper sticker about performing random acts of kindness, decided to adopt this strategy. Every time he felt bad about something in his own life that he couldn't do anything about, he performed an anonymous act of kindness for someone, such as leaving a $5 bill or a note saying "You are loved" in a returned library book, or putting money in someone's expired parking meter. He found that this brightened his mood and gave him hope for the world, as he imagined others "paying it forward," just as he was.

MITZVAH THERAPY

I was giving a keynote address at a large conference in Colorado Springs. Since I was speaking about solution-oriented therapy that day, I decided to begin with the story that inspired me to create solution-oriented therapy. My teacher, Dr. Milton Erickson, had been asked to visit a woman, a relative of one of his patients, who was depressed. She lived in Milwaukee, where Dr. Erickson was scheduled to give a lecture. After his lecture, he visited the woman. It turns out that she had been depressed for the past few years, ever since an illness had confined her to a wheelchair and had thus cut her off from the outside world (this was the 1950s, when the world was not yet wheelchair accessible). After Dr. Erickson arrived at her doorstep, the woman showed him around her rather large house, which she had converted to make it wheelchair accessible. She told him of her life. She lived alone, had never married, had inherited both the house and great deal of money from her family, and was religious. But being in a wheelchair, she had withdrawn from her church because it was so difficult to get out and about.

As he looked around the house, Dr. Erickson found it depressing. She kept the shades drawn and the house seemed big and lonely. The only bright spot on the tour was the final one: the plant nursery, bright and cheery, that was attached to the house and in which she spent most of her waking hours. She loved working with plants and proudly showed Dr. Erickson some new plants, African Violets, which she had gotten going by taking cuttings from existing plants. Dr. Erickson admired her skill with plants and then recommended something that he thought might help with her depression. She was to get a copy of her church newsletter each week and then visit any member of her congregation who had had some significant happy or sad event that week—a birth, a death, an illness, a graduation, an engagement. She was to bring along one of her new African Violet plants as a gift, with her congratulations or condolences. She agreed that perhaps she had been too isolated and wrapped up in her own troubles and assured Dr. Erickson that she would try his suggestion.

That was in the 1950s. In the mid-1970s, when I was studying with Dr. Erickson, he showed me his scrapbook, which contained an article from her local newspaper that was titled "African Violet Queen of Milwaukee dies, mourned by thousands." It turns out that they couldn't fit all the people who wanted to come to her memorial service into the church, since she had touched so many lives over the course of the years in which she had brought these flowers and her presence into their lives.

For me, that story had always illustrated Dr. Erickson's emphasis on finding resources and strengths in people's lives and using these to resolve problems. But I was soon to realize that my emphasis had minimized another aspect of this story.

After I finished my keynote address, there was a keynote speech given by Dr. Sol Gordon. He began: "I'm glad Bill O'Hanlon told that story about the African Violet Queen of Milwaukee, because it has inspired me to throw out the speech I had planned. Instead I'm going to talk to you about the kind of therapy I am doing these days. I call it Mitzvah Therapy."

Dr. Gordon then told the audience a story to illustrate Mitzvah Therapy. (*Mitzvah* is a Hebrew word that means "good deed" or "commandment." Mitzvah Therapy is a therapeutic approach that involves encouraging people to make some sort of social or charitable contribution to help resolve their problems.) A woman had been referred to Dr. Gordon for therapy. She had been abused as a young girl and had been in some years of therapy previously, to no avail. She ate compulsively, was overweight, and spent most of her time working. When she wasn't working, she was alone. As she described her problems and her attempts at finding help, Dr. Gordon told her: "You have already tried psychotherapy. You've given it your best effort and it hasn't worked. I don't think any psychotherapy I offer will be significantly different or better for you. I don't recommend psychotherapy in your case. I recommend Mitzvah

Therapy." She had never heard of this type of therapy, so she asked him to explain.

Dr. Gordon recommended that she find a nearby treatment center for abused and neglected children and volunteer there with her free time. He explained that most treatment centers, due to low budgets and high need, were overwhelmed and would welcome volunteer support. She agreed to give it a try.

When she returned to visit Dr. Gordon in a month's time, she informed him that this Mitzvah Therapy had been profoundly helpful to her. She had discovered that the children needed someone to love and care for them. When she arrived at the door of the treatment center each evening to begin her volunteer shift, the children would run to her, hug her, and want her undivided attention. Staff members were happy to see her, since it gave them a respite in which they could make needed phone calls or write in their charts. She reported that she felt loved and worthwhile for the first time in her life. These children needed her. Dr. Gordon recommended that she continue her Mitzvah Therapy and revisit him in another month.

The next month, the woman reported that another volunteer at the treatment center, Henry, had been watching her interact with the children and was so impressed with her love and commitment to the children that he had asked her out on a date. She told Dr. Gordon that, as he could see, she was no beauty, but Henry, in her view, was downright ugly. Despite that, she had begun to fall in love with him, also moved by his genuine caring for these children. She fell in love with the gentle and good man he was inside. "This Mitzvah Therapy, Dr. Gordon, is incredible. I would recommend it to everyone." She and Henry were eventually married. Months later, she was surprised to hear Dr. Gordon mention that Henry was ugly. "He's not ugly. You must have misunderstood. He's quite a handsome guy." Love is blind, as they say.

When Sol Gordon told that story, it made me realize that I had emphasized the solution-oriented aspects of the African Violet Queen story, but perhaps given short shrift to the service aspects. Dr. Erickson had many cases in which he encouraged people to do something socially useful.

Strategic therapist Cloe Madanes has written about the importance of expiation (making amends) in some cases (Madanes, 1990). For example, if a man had formerly physically abused his wife and then stopped, he might make some reparations to society by donating money regularly to support battered women's services.

It has long been a tenet of the 12-step program for recovery from alcohol dependency both to make amends to people one has harmed and to reach out to support other people who are in recovery.

Sol Gordon also has spoken of an adolescent treatment program for delinquents that set up a project for the residents to spend some of their time being helpers to handicapped and retarded younger kids. The project resulted in less recidivism for the adolescents (that is, fewer return visits to the institution and fewer arrests), but unfortunately the project was discontinued due to bureaucratic changes (Gordon, personal communication, 2002).

A woman who suffered for years from depression told me that there was a pattern to her depression. She would be fine for some months, but then she would enter into a 2-month bout of serious depression that medications and therapy did not seem to do much for. We tried various interventions in therapy and, as with her previous therapy, we discovered that the 2-month bout of depression came no matter what we did. After going through several of these bouts together, I suggested that, since she was a person who was very concerned with others and social causes, we try something different the next time. When she experienced the first stirrings of the next bout of depression, she would do some charitable act. She happened to see a TV report about a young woman in Africa whose family had received a goat from a charity called Heifer International. The gift of a goat, which was in turn passed along to other people in her village, created a cascade of positive changes that resulted in this poor African girl ultimately attending a nice private school and college in the United States, intending to head back to Africa to help people in her old home country after getting her degree. My client decided to make a financial contribution when she began to feel depressed. She felt so good about helping someone else that she forgot about herself for the next few days, and that seemed to make a difference in her level of depression. She decided that, since she wasn't functioning very well during her typical depressions, she would take a week off and volunteer at a local homeless shelter, doing whatever they needed. This again had the same effect. These activities were the first she had ever done that made a difference in the level of depression she experienced. The next bout was shorter-lived and less severe than previous depressive episodes.

Here are some ideas for putting contribution into practice in a clinical setting:

• Ask clients to tell you about some social injustice or victim situation that moves or touches them. Perhaps it's orphans from Africa or the homeless or AIDS sufferers. Or find out about some environmental or world condition that they think is wrong or dangerous, like global warming.
• Every time your clients experience some recurrent problems, suggest that they could do one thing to contribute to the relief of victims' suffering or to right some social or environmental wrong. It may be writing a letter, making a donation of money or time to some charitable group, praying, or some other action they are moved to do.
• Identify something that your clients feel guilty about. Suggest that they anonymously support a cause or

help a victim of something related to whatever they feel they have done wrong.

- Guide your clients to find ways they can be of service or make a contribution that will help them make amends or heal wounds.
- Find out where your clients give of themselves.
- If your clients had to name their most significant contribution to helping others, what would they say?
- If they had to name the cause that they feel most passionate about, what would it be?

IT'S NOT ABOUT YOU

When clients arrive in therapy, they are very concerned about themselves, in large part because their troubles and suffering are capturing their attention. But this attention on the self, reinforced by therapists, can sometimes be counterproductive. Too much attention on the self and on the tiny reality within a therapist's office leaves out the bigger world outside the office and a larger perspective on our problems.

I was counseling a teenager sent by his parents and his school psychologist because he kept getting in fights at school. At the time I first saw him, he was being ex-pelled almost weekly for fighting. I wasn't making much progress with him until several weeks into treatment when I brought up another case with him.

"I'm seeing another kid from a different school who is having a similar problem to yours. He is getting into fights quite a bit. Do you have any advice I can give him since you have dealt with this problem for so long?"

"Sure," he said. "The first thing he's got to do is to count to ten before he hits anybody."

"Okay," I replied, "but what if he says he can't do that?"

"Tell him to think of the consequences and that will help. If he doesn't count to ten, he will be visiting the principal's office; his parents will be down on him and he'll have to come and see a therapist when he'd rather be hanging out with his friends."

I did indeed give my other client his sage advice, but what was so striking was that the client who gave the advice began to improve. He went three weeks without a fight at school. When I asked him how he accomplished this, he said he counted to ten instead of reacting. After the count, he had calmed down enough to decide the consequences weren't worth it, so he walked away from the potential fight.

I tried this technique one other time with good results. I was seeing a young woman who was suffering from a severe case of obsessive-compulsive behavior. One of the components of this problem for her was that she would suffer from delusions. She would develop certain ideas that would become so fixed that she would be blocked from receiving help or leaving her house. A friend once offered her a car so she could obtain a job, but she had to refuse the kind offer since the brand of the car was "Spirit" and she was afraid that a spirit would inhabit her if she drove the car.

At the same time, I was also seeing a young man who was diagnosed with schizophrenia and I asked him if I could get some ideas about how to handle the delusions my other client was suffering from, since he had lots of experience with them. The young woman agreed and he was quite excited to give her tips. He recorded a tape for her with ten suggestions for successfully dealing with and resisting delusions. She found a few of them helpful and responded with a few others she had found helpful that weren't on his list. Both of them improved a bit by helping the other.

I'll give the final word on contribution to British writer W.H. Auden: "We are all here on earth to help others; what on earth the others are here for I don't know."

CHAPTER FOUR

Spirituality
Assessment

There are hundreds of ways to
kneel and kiss the ground.
—RUMI

WHEN I FIRST BEGAN my life as a therapist, I worked
in the area of drug and alcohol treatment. Soon, however,
I transferred to a job in outpatient mental health. I was
surprised to learn that few mental health counselors asked
anything about clients' use of drugs or alcohol or assessed
their family history of drug and alcohol use and abuse. In
chemical dependency treatment, that assessment was routinely done and was important to the treatment.

After a few years, there was more education and awareness in the mental health arena; asking at least something
about current and past drug and alcohol use was an important part of the assessment process. I witnessed a similar dis-

regard and then awakening process with respect to domestic violence, sexual abuse, and issues of racism, sexism, and cross-cultural sensitivities. In each of these areas, therapists got their awareness raised and spent a little time—or at least a question or two—assessing the impact or relevance of these issues, or just listening during the assessment process in case these might be relevant. If they weren't relevant, not much time would have been wasted, but if they were, more time, attention, and energy would be given to the area.

The same can be said about spiritual issues. Perhaps for some of our clients, spiritual issues are not relevant at all; for others, they may be central or crucial. For most, I suspect, they are somewhat relevant but not crucial. Following are some questions you might ask clients in order to assess their spiritual experiences and resources. I would not ask them all, just a few. If there is a vein of gold there to mine, dig deeper. If not, move on to other areas.

You might notice that most of these questions are solution-oriented, that is, they ask about spiritual resources and solutions rather than trauma or problems. That is clearly my bias, so if you have another orientation, you might adjust these questions to make them more problem- or trauma-oriented.

That brings me to another, more general point about these questions. They are not normal questions that have been researched and carefully selected and tested on a scientific basis. I just made them up! So feel free to use them as inspiration rather than to slavishly copy them. They were inspired only by the model in this book and by my curiosity with clients.

In workshops that I give, therapists report several things about the spirituality assessment questions:

1. People tell therapists intimate things about themselves and their families more rapidly than usual. So these questions can be a way of making therapeutic connections with people fairly quickly.
2. The answers often reveal a great deal about family dynamics, which are are often illuminated by the answers to these questions.
3. The answers to these questions often give the client insight into their lives in a different way than psychologically- or emotionally-oriented questions do.
4. These questions, more often than not, evoke strengths and resources that can be readily used to help people cope with or resolve their problems.

SPIRITUAL HISTORY/BACKGROUND

Asking clients about their past can both evoke resources and help you discover or understand any traumas clients might have had related to religion or spirituality. Some possible questions include:

- Have you ever had religious or spiritual beliefs or practices?
- What have been your religious affiliations, if any?

- Have they been helpful in any way?
- Have they been harmful in any way?
- Have you experienced any traumas connected with religion?
- Have you ever felt connected to something more than yourself, like nature, another person, humanity, the universe, or God? When or how?
- What has been your most profound spiritual experience, if any?
- What did each of your parents teach you or show you about religion or spirituality?
- Who else, if anyone, influenced you in regard to religion or spirituality?
- If you ever went away from religion or spirituality and then returned, how did that happen?
- What would you say is the single most profound experience of your life so far?
- What was the period in your life when you most relied on religion, spirituality, or faith for strength?
- What did your family show you in the area of service or compassion?
- What charitable or volunteer activities happened in your family?
- Draw a spiritual and/or religious genogram tracing family connections and experiences with spirituality or religion. This may detail religious affiliations or family history of compassion, contributions/service, and connections.

A client was wrestling with low self-esteem. During the assessment, I asked her about her early religious experiences and she reported having been molested by a priest. She had never told anyone this, as she was so ashamed of it and the priest was still working in her local parish. During the course of therapy, another victim of this priest came forward and made charges against the priest. My client joined in a lawsuit with the person who came forward, as well as with other victims. In the course of meeting with the other victims, their families and lawyers, she felt her self-esteem increasing, as she realized she was now doing something that would help others. She had overcome a significant amount of shame and fear to make her experience known in public.

CURRENT SPIRITUALITY

Where is your client right now in terms of spiritual practices and beliefs? Again, this can provide helpful information about resources to draw upon and connections that already exist that might help people cope with or resolve problems.

Here are some of the questions therapists might use to assess present spiritual practices, resources, and beliefs.

- What do you do or where do you go to "recharge your batteries" when you get a chance?
- What kind of artistic activities do you enjoy (doing or watching)?

- How do you connect with other people?
- How do you connect with something more than yourself?
- Do you think you have a purpose for being alive? If so, what is it?
- Are there any spiritual or religious practices that you do regularly?
- Is there any religious or spiritual figure or activity that you think would be helpful for you in this situation?
- What role, if any, does religion/spirituality play in your life currently?
- What would you say is the single most important ingredient for a spiritual life?
- If you had to pick the most sacred spot you've ever seen, where would it be?
- If you were to name the best aspect of religion, what would it be?
- What do you think is the worst aspect of religion?
- Describe the time or activity that makes you feel the most spiritual.
- Who is the most spiritual person you know?
- Who is the least spiritual person you know?
- If you had to name something that always seems to call or speak to your soul, what would you say?

A client was struggling with addiction and had not found AA helpful despite having tried it many times. In the course of the assessment, I asked him who the most spiritual person he knew was. He mentioned a friend of his who was Quaker. This Quaker friend became our role model as we put together a personalized program for his recovery. The friend:

Read for an hour each day
Did one small thing that would help others each day
Was always calm
Spoke softly
Practiced humility

My client decided that he would try to develop as many of these qualities in his own search for inner peace. He thought that developing inner peace would help reduce his addictive cravings. Indeed, working on developing these qualities did help him increase the time between drug use. While this spiritually based approach did not entirely resolve the addiction, it significantly helped in reducing the problem.

FUTURE SPIRITUAL HOPES AND INTENTIONS

What aspirations do your clients have in regard to their spiritual or religious lives? The following questions are designed to help clients learn about their aspirations and determine whether they are relevant to resolving the problems that brought them to therapy.

• What kind of spiritual or religious activities would you like to do in the future, if any?

- Is there any area of your inner or spiritual life you would like to develop more?
- Is there any spiritual or religious figure that you would consider a model for you? In what way?
- What do you think happens to us when we die?
- What would be the one more thing you could add to your life that you think would make you more spiritual?
- If you were to die tomorrow, who, other than blood relatives, would you want to raise your children?
- If you found out you were terminally ill and could do one thing to put your soul in order, what would it be?

A client of mine kept involving herself in bad relationships and wanted help to stop this destructive pattern. She mentioned offhandedly that her mother had been suggesting to her that she return to the church of her youth. I asked her about her experiences in that church growing up. She reported only positive experiences. I was curious about why she no longer attended that church and she told me that she really wasn't sure. "Why don't you try attending again, then?" I asked. "I guess I will," she replied.

When she returned to her church, she discovered a joy and peace that had been eluding her. She also found some sense of self-love that had been missing through the years she was away from her church. She began to date again and found that relationships were quite different and generally much better.

Before I became so attuned to spiritual assessment and spiritual issues in therapy, I would have let that offhand comment pass without notice.

CHAPTER FIVE

Comparing Religion
and Spirituality

Religion is for people who are afraid of going to hell;
Spirituality is for people who have been there.
—*12*-STEP SAYING

IN THIS BOOK, we have been focused on spirituality,
not religion. But there is a case to be made for the value of
religion in therapy.

Perhaps the best defender of religion is the scholar of
world religions, Huston Smith. In a written debate with
Elizabeth Lesser, Smith (2001) responds to Lesser's ad-
vocacy of borrowing from many spiritual traditions
(which he calls cafeteria-style spirituality) as opposed to
practicing and believing in one religion.

"Religions are time-tested traditions filled with proven
pointers on how to proceed through life" (Smith, 2001).
Because a religion develops over time, it seems a shame

to throw out all that honing and development, he contends. Of course, he knows that religions have their flaws, mainly in that they are conservative and tend to support current social mores and gender roles. "A cow kicks," said Rama Krishna, "but it also gives milk."

"The problem with cafeteria-style spirituality," Smith continues, "is that Saint Ego is often the one making the choices at the salad bar. What tastes good is not always the same as what you need, and an undeveloped ego can make unwise choices."

These days, Smith contends, proponents of spirituality often denigrate religion (not always intentionally, of course). Therefore, in many people's minds spirituality is the good guy and religion the source of evil (fundamentalism, rigidity, shaming, moralizing, pedophilia, justifying wars, and so on). In its defense, Smith points out that religions often organize and carry out local and international relief efforts or charitable activities when people are in need because they're homeless, hungry, or struck by disaster.

Religion also provides moral guidance by helping give people a clear sense of right and wrong. Smith cites the case of President Bill Clinton's affair with Monica Lewinsky when she was a White House intern. Clinton, a religious man, spoke to his minister and acknowledged that he had sinned. When Lewinsky was asked whether she thought she had sinned, she squirmed a bit and said, "I'm not really religious, I'm more spiritual." As her response implies, some "spiritual" people eschew any moral responsibility that religious people find is built in to their spiritual life.

I sometimes ask my clients with religious practices and beliefs, in appropriate situations, what their religion teaches about right and wrong and if they are being congruent with those beliefs. I was working with a couple and the husband was violent toward his wife. When I asked him about his religious beliefs on the subject, he blushed and said that what he was doing wasn't "Christian." I asked him how he managed to live a Christian life in other ways and he told me he had stopped drinking when he had been "born again." To supplement what we were doing in therapy, we decided that he would ask his pastor for help in applying the same powerful self-discipline to his abusive tendencies.

RELIGION VERSUS SPIRITUALITY

Sometimes belonging to and practicing an organized religion can provide essential elements that might be missing if one had merely a spiritual approach or sensibility in life. Let's examine the areas in which religion might provide something spirituality might not.

Ritual

Religion celebrates yearly and seasonal remembrances and other special occasions with repeated rituals. These are actions imbued with meanings that one can count on.

They usually engage the senses: smell (incense, etc.), taste (bread, wine, etc.), sound (singing, chanting, prayer, responsive prayer), sight (special vestments, head covering, etc.), movement (kneeling, facing Mecca, making the sign of the cross, etc.) or touch (rosary beads, prayer books, hymnals, tallis, etc.). Because these rituals have been developed and honed over thousands of years, they are often more powerful and deeper in symbolism than rituals that someone might come up with on his or her own. Rituals also require less thought and planning and give a connection to history and tradition in a way that newly created rituals (or a lack of rituals) do not.

Having grown up Catholic, I only recently learned of the different rituals religious Jews have around death and grief. I find the Jewish rituals a bit more elaborate and, in many ways, better for coping with death and grief. In the first seven days after the death, Jews sit shivah. That means they stop everyday life and gather friends and family around them (this provides needed social support). Mirrors are covered (we are not supposed to be focused on ourselves during this time). The grieved ones are to wear clothes that are ripped (to symbolize their torn and broken hearts; because the grieving are too weak to rip their own clothing, someone else is supposed to rip the clothing for them). There is also a one-year anniversary ritual that involves both prayers and leaving a stone at the headstone of the lost one. At the end of the first year, there is an expectation that the grief will be over if one has observed the rituals. After that, one only does rituals to remember and pray for the departed loved one. Catholicism has some rituals around death, but they pale in comparison to Jewish rituals (this is only my opinion and experience growing up—please don't write to me if you are Catholic and present your compelling evidence for why I have got it wrong).

Group Action and Interaction

Religion involves getting groups of people together for a common purpose or in a common frame of reference. Finding or creating a group of people with like-minded beliefs may be quite difficult. Religions have that aspect built in. Sometimes religion organizes groups of people to do social action or good works. If one tried to organize charitable activities on one's own, it would be more difficult. Religious groups again have a tradition of doing these group social actions, and their motives are usually seen as benevolent.

Religious people and institutions (most notably the Quakers in the United States) were instrumental in creating opposition to slavery in a time when slavery was seen as essential to the economic life of society and hence unchallengeable. The civil rights movement in the United States came out of the churches.

Clear Moral Codes and Guidelines for Behavior

Religions have codes of guidelines (the Ten Commandments, the Torah, the Koran, the Sutras) that have been developed and interpreted for guidance in choosing one's behavior and acting morally. With spirituality, for the most part, one is left to work out these guidelines on one's own.

Atonement After Immoral or Shameful Acts, Thoughts, or Feelings

Religion can help people find their way back to a sense of forgiveness and self-compassion. Religion can help people reconnect with others after they have done, thought, or felt something about which they don't feel right. Religion has worked out ways of atonement and reconciliation over many years. Rituals and guidelines for getting right with the world, other people, and God are often built into religions.

HEALING RELIGIOUS TRAUMAS AND SHAME

Often people who seek our help in therapy have traumas and shame associated with their religious upbringings. This has either invited them away from religion or spirituality or has invited them to a rigid or shaming experience of religion or life in the present. Because therapists have been reluctant to examine this area of spirituality, clients may never have discussed their shaming or traumatic experiences with religion. Clients may never have had a chance to resolve old wounds in this area.

As a result of these difficult earlier experiences with religion, clients sometimes blame God or avoid religion or have the religious transference detailed below. Often clients have not discussed or examined these experiences. It can be helpful at times merely to give clients an opportunity to talk about such experiences in order to have the experiences validated, heard, or to give them a chance to gain a perspective as adults.

The following questions may not be appropriate for all clients. Be careful not to impose these issues on people who are not interested in examining them. But for those who have these issues and for whom they are still alive and influencing them in the present, opening up this area may lead to healing and to an adult experience of healthy spirituality.

- What traumas or shaming experiences have you had related to religion?
- How do you think this has shaped your religious or spiritual life or views?
- In what ways have these traumatic or shaming experiences held you back from the kinds of spiritual or religious practices or life you would like to have?
- What do you imagine might be helpful in healing these old wounds?
- How might these wounds be helpful in energizing your work or spiritual path?
- What is one thing you could do or think that would stand up to or challenge the restraining effects that these wounds have had on you?

RELIGIOUS TRANSFERENCE AND PREMISES ABOUT GOD AND RELIGION

Many clients have been hurt in some ways by religion. They have been shamed by someone in the name of God or religion. Or, they have been physically or sexually abused by someone in the name of God or religion or by some religious figure.

Because these hurts and shamings often happen in childhood, many people develop beliefs or premises about religion, God, or spirituality that do not get updated through the years. Or because they think that these beliefs or practices are intrinsic to religion, they avoid any religious activities or practices. In this section, we'll examine and show how to challenge these old premises or beliefs.

I heard a story about a minister who was traveling on an airplane. He sat next to a woman and they got into a conversation. After talking for a while, she asked him what he did. He said he was a Christian minister. She quickly said, "I don't believe in God." His response was interesting. He had obviously had this conversation with many people, because he wisely asked her, "What is this God in whom you don't believe like?" She said, "He is distant, judgmental, and angry." As the conversation progressed, the minister discovered that the woman's father was, coincidentally, distant, judgmental, and angry and he had promulgated a punitive religious and family atmosphere in the home. This is what I call "religious transference," in which one transfers some experience with an earthly figure to one's conceptions and sense of God. Because God is often viewed as a male figure here in the Western world, this transference often has to do with one's relationship to one's father, but of course it might be with one's mother or some other significant relationship. Some easy questions for therapists to ask their clients in order to investigate this issue of religious transference are:

- Who does this God resemble or remind you of?
- What is this God in whom you don't believe like?

In addition to religious transference, many clients have premises or beliefs about religion or God that haven't been updated since childhood and are a bit generalized or distorted. Here's a list of some of those distorted beliefs that I have come across when talking with clients:

- God is distant.
- God is angry and punitive.
- God doesn't care about me (or people).
- God is male.
- I have to be good or I will be punished.
- God doesn't exist.
- Religion is bad (with a corollary, sometimes, that spirituality is good).
- Religion and spirituality are superstitions or irrational or nonscientific.
- Religion is the opiate of the people.

- Too many terrible things have been done in the name of religion for me to believe or have a religious practice.

If there is a need or a request, therapists can work with clients to challenge these premises and religious transference. Remember, though, that this work is only to be done when clients are suffering from these beliefs and request their therapists' help. It is not the therapists' job to correct their clients as a matter of course because therapists might find these beliefs disturbing, inaccurate, or offensive. Here is a list of considerations and questions for therapists to use to challenge religious premises in a client.

- Identify one or more of your premises about God or religion.
- Where do you think these premises come from?
- Do you think your premise about God or religion is true or accurate, or is it distorted?
- Think of one thing you could do to challenge such a premise or one thing a person with a premise like that would never do. Try that.
- Think of another person you admire or love as a model for the kind of God or religion you would like to have in the world. What would this God or religion be like?

CHAPTER SIX

Solution-Oriented Spirituality

Sometimes I go about pitying myself,
and all along, my soul is being blown by great winds
across the sky.
—OJIBWAY SAYING

I HAVE A THERAPIST FRIEND, Warren Berland. He and I trade consultation services when we get stuck with clinical cases in our therapy practices. He's a creative and optimistic therapist and can always seem to find openings when I am stuck, and I guess I do the same for him.

One day, while talking to him about a case, he casually said, "I would use my 'out-of-the-box' method for that."

"What's that," I asked.

"I've told you about that, haven't I?" he replied. "It's a method for getting people to their spiritual resources, the place that is untouched by trauma and shame, in about five minutes or less."

"No," I replied pointedly, "I think I would have remembered if you had told me about that. What is it?"

Warren had studied many spiritual traditions in the course of his life. Spiritual teachers would often mention that there is a place of grace, of power, connected directly to the source of the spiritual, of God perhaps, that we can all tap into. Unfortunately, most of the time the ability to tap that source requires a lifetime of practice and discipline. Warren had worked out a way to help people connect to it more rapidly. What he told me that day did help with the particular case, but it also gave me a simple method that I have used since then. I have changed and adapted it in my own way, but the essence comes from Warren's work (Berland, 1998). There are three simple steps to this method, which I have called Solution-Oriented Spirituality.

THREE STEPS TO SOLUTION-ORIENTED SPIRITUALITY

1. Help Clients Identify a Problem or Stuck Place in Their Lives

Have clients recall a recurring problem or difficult place in their lives. Have them connect experientially with that problem, that is, how it felt or feels in their body.

A therapist's typical set of instructions might be something like:

Think of the problem now. If you need to go inside or close your eyes to do this, you can do so now. The main thing is that I would like to invite you to really experience the frustration or difficulty of the problem in your body and emotions before helping you to resolve it. What sort of feeling do you get in your body when you connect with the problem or when you are having the problem? What feelings do you have? How do you relate to others or yourself? What kind of thinking are you doing during this problem time?

2. Help Clients to Revisit Spiritual Moments or Times and Recreate or Reconnect to the Experience

Have clients recall a time or phase in their lives when they felt connected, free, flowing, alive, energetic, expansive, or resourceful.

A therapist's typical set of instructions might be something like:

Now I want you to set the problem aside and connect with another kind of experience. This time, again, I would like to invite you to connect with this experience in your body or your emotions, to somehow bring it to life within your experience right now. Can you connect to a time when you felt really resourceful or okay? Or perhaps a time when you felt connected to yourself in a good way or connected to something bigger? It might be a time when you felt flowing or loving or at peace or joyful. It might be a particular moment or a phase in your life. But the main thing is to remember what that felt like or feels like in your body. What kind of sense did you or do you have in your body as you reconnect with that positive experience? One person doing this said she remembered this time in her life as "golden" and that she felt like she had "honey flowing through her veins." Can you come up with any images that come to your mind about this connected time or feeling? As much as possible, connect to it. What was your thinking like at that moment or those times? How did you relate to others during that moment or those times?

3. Help Clients to Bring That Sense of Spirituality to Any Situation in Which They Are Having Current Difficulty or Anticipate Having Difficulty in the Future

After helping clients to recreate the spiritual experience, bring it to any current or future situation in which the clients have felt stuck, petty, selfish, or frightened. Have the clients imagine in detail how they would feel in their body and what their thinking, actions, and ways of relating to others would be from that more expansive, spiritual place.

Here's what a therapist might say:

Now reexamine the problem from this more connected or peaceful or joyful place. What do you notice that is different as you are examining it from this new place? What else has changed, if anything, from this perspective? Is the problem even still a problem from here? What choices or options are available to you from this place that weren't obvious or available from the problem place? How would you relate to others differently from this place in regard to the problem? Does the problem appear any smaller or farther away? Anything else you notice or know from this place?

This process usually only takes 5 minutes or so, so if it doesn't work, there is little lost. But if it does have an impact, then I have found that the effect is often profound and that clients can refer back to this resource again and again as they face this and other problems. Some of my clients have even permanently solved their problem using this process. Five minutes to resolve a problem? That is a pretty good bang for the buck, as the saying goes.

To give you an example of using this method in therapy, once I was working with a couple who were working through the aftereffects of her having had an affair. The husband was devastated when he learned about the affair, but after some months of tension about divorce and separation, they decided to stay together. Then the husband began to make regular sarcastic comments when they would pass a man on the street. "Do you want to have sex with that one, too?" "Oh, he's hot. I wonder if his **** is bigger than mine." These comments led to arguments and bitterness between the couple and made them both reconsider their decision to stay together.

In couples therapy, I asked them where they would be if they could be anywhere in the world right now. They both chose the Cayman Islands. They spoke about the beautiful weather, the amazing beaches and ocean, and the feeling of peace they had found there on several trips.

I asked them to imagine being in the Caymans for several weeks and having that sense of peace and joy. When they were able to access that sense, I asked them both to imagine a scene in which they would have gotten into one of their typical bitter exchanges. The husband said that he would realize that he was frightened and bitter and would tell his wife he was having trouble and drop the sarcastic remarks. The wife said that she would recognize that her husband was feeling upset and not react to his comments, but instead squeeze his hand and tell him she was sorry for what she had done and was sorry he was feeling so bad. The next time such an opportunity arose, the husband restrained himself and they didn't fall into the usual difficulty. He slipped a few times after that, and most of those times the wife was able to respond with her spiritually based response, with love, compassion, and regret. The old pattern gradually fell away.

I call this solution-oriented spirituality since all you as the therapist are doing is reminding or reevoking a spiritual-type experience for the clients. They then can use this evoked resource to help resolve the problem. You don't need to know much about how the problem arose or give much guidance about how to use the evoked resource, since it is almost always obvious to clients how to do so. For more about the solution-oriented method, see Berland (1998).

THE LITTLE SELF AND THE BIGGER SELF

I have become identified by many in the field of psychotherapy as a brief solution-oriented therapist, so it may come as a surprise to those who have seen me in this light that I have written this book on spirituality. But for me, there is no contradiction or leaving behind of my solution-orientation in these pages. I see this as an expansion and elaboration of the same sense of clients that led me to develop and advocate for solution-oriented approaches. I have the sense that clients are more than they appear (sick, crazy, resourceless, or powerless) when they arrive in therapists' offices. I never believed that this was all there was to clients. Traditional therapy training, unfortunately, often reinforces this "small" view of people. I had another sense of clients and believed that they were capable, healthy, and had possibilities that weren't apparent in the midst of their problems.

When clients arrive in a therapist's office, they are often so demoralized by the problems and their effects that they have forgotten their resources and gone "small."

My friend and colleague Stephen Gilligan (1997) has a funny way of putting it. He says that clients are in a "symptom trance," where they have been convinced by the symptom that things are hopeless and that they have no power to change their situations. They often then inadvertently invite the therapist into the same kind of trance.

I am depression, they seem to intone. *When you look at me, you will see only hopelessness. I have always been only depressed and powerless. I will only be the same or worse in the future. Go deeply and deeply into this "depression trance" and see nothing else.*

If the therapist is entranced by this bleak view of their clients, therapy usually doesn't go well. I am rarely caught by it since I remember that clients have resources far greater within and beyond themselves. I have a faith in something greater, so change isn't merely determined by how skillful I am or what kind of personal history clients have had or how things appear to be at the moment. Things only *seem* bleak or hopeless. There is more to the story, more available to clients at every moment that they have forgotten or not tapped into.

This view was part of what gave rise to the brief, solution-oriented view that I have written about and taught for so many years.

Clients often operate as if the current patterns of thinking, perception, meaning, action, and interaction are the limits of their world. But if therapy can get them to step outside these usual restrictions and limitations, new possibilities arise and problems can often be resolved relatively quickly and easily.

I have called this stepping outside the typical patterns "changing the viewing" and "changing the doing." The quotations that illustrate this well are: "There is nothing as dangerous as an idea when it is the only one you have" (Emile Chartier) and "Insanity is doing the same thing over and over again and expecting different results" (a 12-step saying). The situation is akin to the story about the polar bear that was limited by a short length of 6-foot chain to which he was tethered while his enclosure at the zoo was being completed. After being released from the chain, he continued to limit his pacing back and forth to this 6-foot length. There is a big wide world of possibilities and we often limit ourselves to a small circle of action and perception. I firmly hold that, regarding their problems, clients can step outside the small circles of stuckness within which they have been moving.

Author Marianne Williamson (1996) has written (a passage often attributed to Nelson Mandela, since he apparently quoted it in his inaugural address):

> Our deepest fear is not that we are inadequate. Our deepest fear is that we are powerful beyond measure. It is our light, not our darkness, that most frightens us. We ask ourselves, "Who am I to be brilliant, gorgeous, talented, and fabulous?" Actually, who are you NOT to be? You are a child of God. Your "playing small" does not serve the world. There is nothing enlightened about shrinking so that other people don't feel insecure around you. We were born to make manifest the glory of God that is within us. It is not just in some of us. It is in everyone. As you let your light shine, you unconsciously give other people permission to do the same. As you are liberated from your own fears, your presence automatically liberates others.

Or as my friend and colleague Stephen Gilligan is fond of saying: "You are up to something big!" You may be up to something big, but at times you go small. One of those times is when you are beset with problems.

When clients arrive with their problems and they have gone small inside themselves, I gently steer them toward realizing that there are more resources with which they can connect inside. There is their deeper self and wisdom, knowledge that is beyond the conscious, rational, ego-identified self. They also live in a body, with its wisdom and resources.

The picture might look like this:

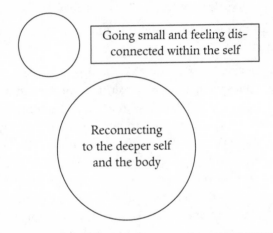

Going small and feeling disconnected within the self

Reconnecting to the deeper self and the body

FIGURE **6.1.** RECONNECTING WITH PERSONAL RESOURCES.

Likewise, when clients have disconnected from their social resources, through the next two of the seven pathways, we as therapists can help remind them of and evoke connections to others, including their communities. Graphically, it could look something like Figure 6.2.

Finally, we as therapists can help our clients to connect with something bigger than personal and interpersonal resources, and to draw upon the transpersonal, or

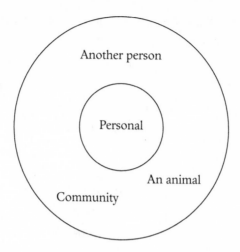

FIGURE **6.2.** RECONNECTING TO INTERPERSONAL RESOURCES.

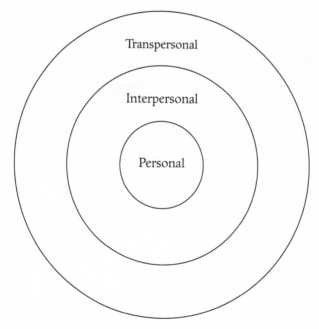

FIGURE **6.3.** RECONNECTING TO TRANSPERSONAL RESOURCES.

"beyond people." This realm includes the final three pathways to connection: nature, art, and God or a higher power.

Figure 6.3 gives the overview of the three areas in which we search in a spiritual approach for resources and connection: the personal, the interpersonal, and the transpersonal.

I hope this book has illustrated useful methods for evoking and implementing freedom from suffering and unworkable patterns. May you find many pathways to spirituality in your own life and in the lives of your clients.

Spirituality
and Therapy
Reading List

Alport, G. (1950). *The individual and his religion.* New York: Macmillan & Co.

Alter, R. M. & Alter, J. (2000). *The transformative power of crisis: Our journey to psychological healing and spiritual awakening.* New York: Regan Books. (Paperback title: *How long til my soul gets it right?*)

Anderson, D. A. & Worthen, D. (1997). Exploring a fourth dimension: Spirituality as a resource for the couple therapist. *Journal of Marital and Family Therapy, 23*(1), 3–12.

Aponte, H. J. (1996). Political bias, moral values, and spirituality in the training of psychotherapists. *Bulletin of the Menninger Clinic, 60*(4), 488–502.

Aziz, R. (1990). *C. G. Jung's psychology of religion and synchronicity.* Albany: State University of New York Press.

Bach, R. (1977). *Illusions: The adventures of a reluctant messiah.* New York: Delacorte.

Barry, W. A. (1977). Prayer in pastoral care: A contribution from the tradition of spiritual direction. *The Journal of Pastoral Care, 31*(2), 91–96.

Beck, J. R. (2003). Self and soul: Exploring the boundary between psychotherapy and spiritual formation. *Journal of Psychology and Theology, 31*(1), 24–37.

Becvar, D. (1997). *Soul healing: A spiritual orientation in counseling and therapy.* New York: Basic Books.

Bellingham, R., Cohen, B., Jones T., & Spaniol, L. (1989). Spirituality and sense of well-being in persons with AIDS. *Holistic Nursing Practice, 3*(4), 16–25.

Benor, D. J. (1993). Spiritual healing, assuming the spiritual is real. *Advances, 9*(4),22–30.

Berenson, D. (1990). A systemic view of spirituality: God and twelve-step programs as resources in family therapy. *Journal of Strategic and Systemic Therapies, 9,* 50–70.

Bergin, A. E. (1991). Values and religious issues in psychotherapy and mental health. *American Psychologist, 46,* 394–403.

Bergin, A. E., & Jensen, J. (1990). Religiosity of psychotherapists: A national survey. *Psychotherapy, 27,* 3–7.

Bidwell, D. R. (2004). *Short-term spiritual guidance: A contemporary approach to a classic discipline.* In Howard W. Stone (Ed.), *Creative Pastoral Care and Counseling Series.* Minneapolis: Fortress.

Boyd-Franklin, N., & Walker Lockwood, T. (1999). Spirituality and religion: Implications for psychotherapy with African-American clients and families. In F. Walsh (Ed.), *Spirituality resources in family therapy* (pp. 90–103). New York: Guilford Press.

Braverman, E. R. (1987). The religious medical model: Holy medicine and the spiritual behavior inventory. *Southern Medical Journal, 80*(4), 415–420.

Brgadon, E. (1993). *A Sourcebook for helping people with spiritual problems.* Aptos, CA: Lightening Up Press.

Brown, H. P., Peterson, J. H., & Cunningham, O. (1988). Rationale and theoretical basis for a behavioral/cognitive approach to spirituality. *Alcoholism Treatment Quarterly, 5*(1/2), 47–59.

Burke, M. T. & Miranti, J. G. (Eds.) (1995). *Counseling: The spiritual dimension.* Alexandria, VA: American Counseling Association.

Burkhardt, M. A. (1989). Spirituality: An analysis of a concept. *Holistic Nursing Practice, 3*(3), 69–76.

Butler, M. H., Gardner, B. C., & Bird, M. H. (1998). Not just a time-out: Change dynamics of prayer for religious couples in conflict situations. *Family Process, 37,* 451–478.

Butler, M., & Harper, J. (1994). The divine triangle: God in the marital system of religious couples. *Family Process, 33,* 277–286.

Campbell, J. (1988). *The Power of Myth.* New York: Viking.

Canda, E. R. (1986). A conceptualization of spirituality for social work: Its issues and implications. (Doctoral dissertation, The Ohio State University, 1986). *Dissertation Abstracts International, 47*(7-A), 2737–2738. (UMI No. 8625190)

Canda, E. R. (1988a). Conceptualizing spirituality for social work: Insights from diverse perspectives. *Social Thought, 14*(1), 30–46.

Canda, E. R. (1988b). Spirituality, religious diversity, and social work practice. *Social Casework, 69*(4), 238–247.

Canda, E. R. (1990a). Afterward: Spirituality re-examined. *Spirituality and Social Work Communicator, 1*(1), 13–14.

Canda, E. R. (1990b). An holistic approach to prayer for social work practice. *Social Thought, 16*(3), 3–13.

Canda, E. R. (1990c). Spirituality, diversity, and social work values. In J. J. Kattakayam (Ed.), *Contemporary social issues.* Trivandrum, India: University of Kerala Press.

Canda, E. R. (1995). Retrieving the soul of social work. *Society for Spirituality and Social Work Newsletter, 2*(2), 5–8.

Canda, E. R. (1997). Do religion and spirituality have a significant place in the core HBSE curriculum? Yes. In M. Bloom & W. C. Klein (Eds.), *Controversial issues in human behavior in the social environment* (pp. 172–177, 183–184). Boston: Allyn and Bacon.

Carr, E. W. & Morris, T. (1996). Spirituality and patients with advanced cancer: A social work response. *Journal of Psychosocial Oncology, 14*(1), 71–81.

Carroll M. M. (1997). Spirituality and clinical social work: Implications of past and current practices. *Arete, 22*(1), 25–34.

Carroll, S. (1991). Spirituality and purpose in life in alcoholism recovery. *Journal of Studies in Alcohol,* May, 297–301.

Cashwell, C. S. (2001). The inclusion of spiritual process in counseling and perceived counselor effectiveness. *Counseling and Values, 45*(2), 145–154.

Clark, I. (Ed.) (2001). *Psychosis and spirituality: Exploring the new frontier.* London: Whurr Pub.

Coehlho, P. (1993). *The Alchemist: A fable about following your dream.* San Francisco: HarperSanFrancisco.

Cornett, C. (1992). Toward a more comprehensive personology: Integrating a spiritual perspective into social work practice. *Social Work, 37*(2), 101–102.

Cornett, C. (1998). *The soul of psychotherapy: Recapturing the spiritual dimension in the therapeutic encounter.* New York: The Free Press.

Corrington, J. E., Jr. (1989). Spirituality and recovery: Relationships between levels of spirituality, contentment, and stress during recovery from alcoholism in AA. *Alcoholism Treatment Quarterly, 6*(3/4), 151–160.

Cortwright, B. (1997). *Psychotherapy and spirit: Theory and practice in transpersonal psychotherapy.* Albany: State University of New York Press.

Cowley, A. S. (1993). Transpersonal social work: A theory for the 1990s. *Social Work, 38*(5), 527–534.

Cox, D. (1985). The missing dimension in social work practice. *Australian Social Work, 38*(4), 5–11.

DiBlasio, F. (1988). Integrative strategies for family therapy with evangelical Christians. *Journal of Psychology and Theology, 16,* 127–134.

Elkins, D. N., Hedstrom, L. J., Hughes, L. L., Leaf, J. A., & Saunders, C. (1988). Toward a humanistic-phenomenological spirituality. *Journal of Humanistic Psychology, 28*(4), 5–18.

Ellison, C. W. (1983). Spiritual well-being: Conceptualization and measurement. *Journal of Psychology and Theology, 11,* 330–340.

Engquist, D. E. (1997). Occupational therapists' beliefs and practices with regard to spirituality and therapy. *American Journal of Occupational Therapy, 51*(3), 173–180.

Everts, J. F. (1994). Including spirituality in counselor education: Issues for consideration, with illustrative reference to a New Zealand example. *International Journal for the Advancement of Counseling, 17*(4), 291–302.

Fahlberg, L. L. (1991). Exploring spirituality and consciousness with an expanded science: Beyond the ego with empiricism, phenomenology, and contemplation. *American Journal of Health Promotion, 5*(4), 273–281.

Faiver, C., Ingersoll, R. E., Obrien, E., & McNally, C. (2001). *Explorations in counseling and spirituality: Philosophical, practical, and personal reflections.* Belmont, CA: Brooks/Cole/Wadsworth/ Thompson.

Fehring, R. J., Brennan, P. F., & Keller, M. L. (1987). Psychological and spiritual well-being in college students. *Research in Nursing and Health, 10,* 391–398.

Ferrucci, P. (1982). *What we may be: Techniques for psychological and spiritual growth through psychosynthesis.* LA, CA: J. P. Tarcher.

Fleischman, P. (1993). *Spiritual aspects of psychiatric practice.* Cleveland, SC: Bonne Chance Press.

Flemons, D. (1991). *Completing distinctions: Interweaving the ideas of Gregory Bateson and Taoism into a unique approach to therapy.* Boston: Shambhala.

Fowler, J. W. (1981). *Stages of faith: The psychology of human development and the quest for meaning.* San Francisco: Harper and Row.

Frame, M. W. (1996). Counseling African Americans: Integrating spirituality in therapy. *Counseling Values, 4*(1), 16–28.

Frankl, V. E., (1967). *Psychotherapy and existentialism.* New York: Washington Square Press.

Gabriel, G. P. (1994). How do you get the spiritual part of the program? *Journal of Ministry in Addiction and Recovery, 1*(1), 41–46.

Gartner, J., Larson, D. B., & Allen, G. (1991). Religious commitment and mental health: A review of the empirical literature. *Journal of Psychology and Theology, 19*(1), 6–25.

Glenn, N. D. & Weaver, C. N. (1978). A multivariate, multi-survey study of marital happiness. *Journal of Marriage and the Family, 40,* 269–282.

Glynn, P. (1997). *God: The evidence.* Rockland, CA: Prima.

Green, A. (1987). Spirituality. In A. A. Cohen and P. Mendes-Flohr (Eds.), *Contemporary Jewish religious thought: Original essays on critical concepts, movements, and beliefs* (pp. 903–908). New York: Free Press.

Griffith, B. A. & Griggs, J. C. (2001). Religious identity status as a model to understand, assess, and interact with client spirituality. *Counseling and Values, 46*(1), 14–26.

Griffith, J. L., & Griffith, M. E. (1992). Therapeutic change in religious families: Working with the God-construct (pp. 63–86). In L. Burton (Ed.). *Religion and the family: When God helps.* Binghamton, New York: Haworth Press.

Griffith, J. L., & Griffith, M. E. (2002). *Encountering the sacred in psychotherapy: How to talk to people about their spiritual lives.* New York: Guilford Press.

Grof S., & Grof, C. (Eds.) (1989). *Spiritual emergency: When personal transformation becomes a crisis.* New York: J. P. Tarcher/Putnam.

Haley, J. (1994). Zen and the art of therapy. *The Family Therapy Networker, 18*(1).

Halstead, M. T., & Fernsler, J. I. (1994). Coping strategies of long-term cancer survivors. *Cancer Nursing, 17*(2), 94–100.

Hillman, J. (1996). *The soul's code: In search of character and calling.* New York: Random House.

Hodge, D. R. (2000). Spiritual ecomaps: A new diagrammatic tool for assessing marital and family spirituality. *Journal of Marital and Family Therapy, 26,* 229–240.

Hodge, D. R. (2001). Spiritual assessment: A review of major qualitative methods and a new framework for assessing spirituality. *Social Work, 46,* 193–288.

Huxley, A. (1945). *The perennial philosophy*. New York: Harper and Brothers Publishing.

Jagers, R. J. & Smith, P. (1996). Further examination of the spirituality scale. *Journal of Black Psychology, 22*(4), 429–442.

Jenkins, R. A. (1995). Religion and spirituality as resources for coping with cancer. *Journal of Psychosocial Oncology, 13*(1/2), 51–74.

Johnson, C. V., & Hayes, J. A. (2003). Troubled spirits: Prevalence and predictors of religious and spiritual concerns among university students and counseling center clients. *Journal of Counseling Psychology, 50*(4), 409–419.

Jordan, J. (1985). Paradox and polarity: The Tao of family therapy. *Family Process, 24,* 165–174.

Kahle, P. A. & Robbins, J. M. (2004). *The power of spirituality in therapy: Integrating spiritual and religious beliefs in mental health practice.* Binghamton, New York: Haworth Press.

Kauffman, J. H. (1979). Social correlates of spiritual maturity among North American Mennonites. In D. Moberg (Ed.), *Spiritual wellbeing and sociological perspectives* (pp. 237–254). Washington, D.C.: University Press of America.

Kelly, E. W. (1995). *Spirituality and religion in counseling and psychotherapy: Diversity in theory and practice.* Alexandria, VA: American Counseling Association.

Kersting, K. (2003). Religion and spirituality in the treatment room. *Monitor on Psychology,* December, pp. 40–42.

Kilpatrick, A. C. & Holland, T. P. (1990). Spiritual dimensions of practice. *The Clinical Supervisor, 8*(2), 125–140.

Koenig, H. J. (1999). *The Healing Power of Faith.* New York: Simon and Schuster.

Koenig, H. G., Cohen, H. J., Blazer, D. G., Kudler, H. S., Krishnan, K. R. R., & Sibert, T. E. (1995). Cognitive symptoms of depression and religious coping in elderly medical patients. *Psychosomatics, 36,* 369–375.

Koenig, H. G, George. L. K, & Peterson, B. L. (1998). Religiosity and remission of depression in medically ill older patients. *American Journal of Psychiatry, 155*(4), 536–542.

Koenig, H. G., Cohen, H. J., Blazer, D. G., Pieper, C., & Meador, K. G., Shelp, F., Goli, V., & DiPasquale, R. (1992). Religious coping and depression in elderly hospitalized medically ill men. *American Journal of Psychiatry, 149,* 1693–1700.

Koenig, H. G., Ford, S., George, L. K., Blazer, D. G., & Meador, K. G. (1993). Religion and anxiety disorder: An examination and comparison of associations in young, middle-aged, and elderly adults. *Journal of Anxiety Disorders, 7,* 321–342.

Koenig, H. G., George, L. K., Meador, K. G., Blazer, D. G., & Dyke, P. (1994). Religious affiliation and psychiatric disorder in Protestant baby boomers. *Hospital and Community Psychiatry, 45,* 586–596.

Koenig, H. G., George, L. K., Meador, K. G., Blazer, D. G., & Ford, S. M. (1994). The relationship between religion and alcoholism in a sample of community-dwelling adults. *Hospital and Community Psychiatry, 45,* 225–231.

Koenig, H. G., Hays, J. C., George, L. K., & Blazer, D. G., Larson, D. B., & Landerman, L. R. (1997). Modeling the cross-sectional relationships between religion, physical health, social support, and depressive symptoms. *American Journal of Geriatric Psychiatry, 5,* 131–143.

Koss, J. D. (1987). Expectations and outcomes for patients given mental health care or spiritualist healing in Puerto Rico. *American Journal of Psychiatry, 144*(1), 56–61.

Laing, R. D. (1989). Transcendental experience in relation to religion and psychosis. In S. Grof & C. Grof (Eds.), *Spiritual Emergency.* New York: Putnam.

Larson, D. B., & Larson, S. S. (1992). *The forgotten factor in physical and mental health: What does the research show?* Rockville, MD: National Institute for Healthcare Research.

Larson, D. B., & Wilson, W. P. (1980). Religious life of alcoholics. *Southern Medical Journal, 73*(6), 723–727.

Leskowitz, E. (1993). Spiritual healing, modern medicine, and energy. *Advances, 9*(4), 50–53.

Levin, J. S. (1993). Esoteric vs. exoteric explanations for findings linking spirituality and health. *Advances, 9*(4), 54-56.

Ley, D. C. (1988). Spirituality and hospice care. Special issue: Cultural and religious perspectives of death. *Death Studies*, *12*(2), 101–110.

Lloyd, M. (1997). Dying and bereavement, spirituality and social work in a market economy of welfare. *British Journal of Social Work*, *27*(2), 175–190.

Loch, R. B., & Hughes, R. H. (1985). Religion and youth substance abuse. *Journal of Religion and Health*, *24*(3), 197–180.

Lovinger, R. (1994). *Working with religious issues in therapy*. Northvale, NJ: Jason Araonson.

Mahoney, A. M., Pargament, K. I., Jewell, T., Swank, A. B., Scott, E., Emery, E., et al. (1999). Marriage and the spiritual realm: The role of proximal and distal religious constructs in marital functioning. *Journal of Family Psychology*, *13*, 321–338.

Maslow, A. (1964). *Religion, values and peak experiences*. Cleveland: Ohio State University Press.

Mathew, R. J., Georgi, J., Wilson, W. H., & Mathew, V. (1996). A retrospective study of the concept of spirituality as understood by recovering individuals. *Journal of Substance Abuse Treatment*, *13*(1), 67–73.

Mathew, R. J., Mathew, V. G., Wilson, W. H., & Georgi, J. M. (1995). Measurement of materialism and spiritualism in substance abuse research. *Journal of Studies on Alcohol*, *56*(4), 470–475.

May, G. G. (1992). *Care of mind, care of spirit: A psychiatrist explores spiritual direction*. San Francisco: HarperCollins.

McCarthy, H. (1995). Integrating spirituality into rehabilitation in a technocratic society. *Rehabilitation Education*, *9*(2/3), 87–95.

McDowell, D., Galanter, M., Goldfarb, L., & Lifshutz, H. (1996). Spirituality and the treatment of the dually diagnosed: An investigation of patient and staff attitudes. *Journal of Addictive Diseases*, *15*(2), 55–68.

McGrath, P. (1997). Putting spirituality on the agenda: Hospice research findings on the "ignored" dimension. *Hospice Journal*, *12*(4), 1–14.

Miller, J. S. (1990). Mental illness and spiritual crisis: Implications for psychiatric rehabilitation. *Psychosocial Rehabilitation Journal*, *14*(2), 29–47.

Miller, M. E. and West, A. N. (Eds.) (2000). *Spirituality, ethics, and relationship in adulthood: Clinical and theoretical explorations*. Madison, WI: Psychosocial Press.

Miller, W. R. (Ed.) (1999). *Integrating spirituality into treatment: Resources for practitioners.* Washington, D.C.: American Psychological Association.

Millison, M. B. (1995). A review of the research on spiritual care and hospice. *The Hospice Journal*, *10*(4), 3–18.

Mitchell, S. (1996). *The official guide to American attitudes*. Ithaca, New York: New Strategist Publications, Inc.

Moberg, D. O., & Brusek, P. M. (1978). Spiritual wellbeing: A neglected subject in quality of life research. *Social Indicators Research*, *5*, 303–323.

Molino, A. (Ed.) (1988). *The couch and the tree: Dialogues in psychoanalysis and Buddhism.* New York: American Psychological Association and Work Projects Administration.

Moore, R. J. (2003). Spiritual assessment. *Social Work*, *48*(4), 558–561.

Moules, N. (2000). Postmodernism and the sacred: Reclaiming connection in our greater-than-human worlds. *Journal of Marital and Family Therapy, 26*, 229–240.

Nathanson, I. G. (1995). Divorce and women's spirituality. *Journal of Divorce and Remarriage*, *22*(3/4), 179–188.

O'Brien, R.Y. (1994). Spirituality in treatment programs for addicts. *Journal of Ministry in Addiction and Recovery, 1*(1), 69–76.

O'Connell, T. (1991). Michigan historian: Spirituality at the heart of AA's success. *The U.S. Journal of Drug and Alcohol Dependence, 15*(2).

Oxman, T. E., Freeman, D. H., & Manheimer, E. D. (1995). Lack of social participation or religious strength and comfort as risk factors for death after cardiac surgery in the elderly. *Psychosomatic Medicine, 57*(1), 5–15.

Paloutzian, R., & Ellison, S. (1982). Loneliness, spiritual well-being, and quality of life. In L. Peplau and D. Perlman (Eds.), *Loneliness: A sourcebook of current theory, research and therapy* (pp. 224–237). New York: John Wiley and Sons.

Patterson, J., Hayworth, M., Turner, C., & Raskin, M. (2000). Spiritual issues in family therapy: A graduate level course. *Journal of Marital and Family Therapy, 26*, 199–210.

Perry, J. W. (1999). *Trials of the visionary mind: Spiritual emergence and the renewal process.* Albany: State University of New York Press.

Peterson, E. A., & Nelson, K. (1987). How to meet your clients' spiritual needs. *Journal of Psychosocial Nursing, 25*(5), 34–39.

Pressman, P., Lyons, J. S., Larson, D. B., & Strain, J. J. (1990). Religious belief, depression, and ambulatory status in elderly women with broken hips. *American Journal of Psychiatry, 147*(6), 758–760.

Prest. L., & Keller, J. F. (1993). Spirituality and family therapy: Spiritual beliefs, myths, and metaphors. *Journal of Marital and Family Therapy, 19*(2), 137–148.

Prest, L., Russel, R., & D'Souza, H. (1999). Spirituality and religion in training, practice, and personal development. *Journal of Family Therapy, 21*, 60–77.

Prezioso, F. A. (1987). Spirituality in the recovery process. *Journal of Substance Abuse Treatment, 4*, 233–238.

Propst, R. (1998). *Psychotherapy in a religious framework: Spirituality in the emotional healing process.* New York: Human Sciences Press.

Reed, P. G. (1987). Spirituality and well-being in terminally ill hospitalized adults. *Research Nursing and Health, 10*, 335–344.

Reed, P. G. (1992). An emerging paradigm for the investigation of spirituality in nursing. *Research in Nursing and Health, 15*, 349–357.

Richards, P. S., & Bergin, A. E. (1997). *A spiritual strategy for counseling and psychotherapy.* Washington, D.C.: American Psychological Association.

Richards, P. S., & Bergin, A. E. (2000). *Handbook of psychotherapy and religious diversity.* Washington, D.C.: American Psychological Association.

Ross, J. (1994). Working with patients within their religious contexts: Religion, spirituality, and the secular therapist. *Journal of Systemic Therapies, 13*, 7–15.

Rotz, E., Russell, C., & Wright, D. (1993). The therapist who is perceived as "spiritually correct": Strategies for avoiding collusion with the "spiritually one-up" spouse. *Journal of Marital and Family Therapy, 19*, 369–375.

Sansone, R., Khatain, K., & Rodenhauser, P. (1990). The role of religion in psychiatric education: A national survey. *Academic Psychiatry, 14*, 34–38.

Schaler, J. A. (1996). Spiritual thinking in addiction-treatment providers: The spiritual belief scale. *Alcoholism Treatment Quarterly, 14*(3), 7–33.

Schaub, R. (1995). Alternative health and spiritual practices. *Alternative Health Practitioner, 1*(1), 35–38.

Scotton, B. W., Chinen, A. B., & Battista, J. R. (Eds.) (1996). *Textbook of transpersonal psychiatry and psychology.* New York: Basic Books.

Seaward, B. L. (1995). Reflections on human spirituality for the worksite. *American Journal of Health Promotion, 9*(3), 165–168.

Sermabeikian, P. (1994). Our clients, ourselves: The spiritual perspective and social work practice. *Social Work, 39*(2), 178–183.

Shafranske, E. P. (1984). Factors associated with the perception of spirituality in psychotherapy. *Journal of Transpersonal Psychology, 16*(2), 231–241.

Shafranske, E. P. (Ed.) (1996). *Religion and the practice of psychology.* Washington, D.C.: American Psychological Association.

Shorto, R. (1999). *Saints and madmen: How pioneering psychiatrists are creating a new science of the soul.* New York: Henry Holt.

Sorenson, R. (2004). *Minding spirituality.* Hillsdale, NJ: Analytic Press.

Sovotsky, S. (1998). *Words from the soul: Time, east/west spirituality and psychotherapeutic narrative.* Albany: State University Press of New York.

Spangler, D. (2001). *Blessing: The art and the practice.* New York: Riverhead.

Spaniol, L. (1985). Divorce and spirituality. *Studies in Formative Spirituality, 6*(3), 399–405.

Sperry, L. (2001). *Spirituality in clinical practice: Incorporating the spiritual in psychotherapy and counseling.* Philadelphia, PA: Brunner-Routledge.

Spielman, E. (1979). *The mighty atom: The life and times of Joseph L. Greenstein; Biography of a superhuman.* New York: The Viking Press.

Stack, S. (1983). The effect of the decline in institutionalize religion on suicide, 1954–1978. *Journal for the Scientific Study of Religion, 22,* 239–252.

Stewart, S., & Gale, J. (1994). On hallowed ground: Marital therapy with couples on the religious right. *Journal of Systemic Therapies, 13,* 16–25.

Sullivan, W. P. (1993). It helps me to be a whole person: The role of spirituality among the mentally challenged. *The Psychosocial Rehabilitation Journal, 16*(3), 125–134.

Taylor, E. (1999). *Shadow culture: Psychology and spirituality in America.* Washington, D.C.: Counterpoint.

Thornton, E. E. (1977). Spirituality and pastoral care. *The Journal of Pastoral Care, 31*(2), 73–75.

Titone, A. (1991). Spirituality and psychotherapy in social work practice. *Spirituality and Social Work Commentary, 2*(1), 7–9.

Tubesing, D. A. (1980). Stress, spiritual outlook, and health. *Journal of Specialized Pastoral Care, 3,* 17–23.

Ullery, E. (2004). Consideration of a spiritual role in sex and sex therapy. *The Family Journal, 12*(1), 78–81.

Van Hook, M., Hugan, B., & Aguilar, M. (2001). *Spirituality within religious traditions in social work.* Pacific Grove, CA: Brooks/Cole.

Verge, C. (1992). Foundations for a spiritually based psychotherapy. In L. Burton (Ed.), *Religion and the family: When God helps* (pp. 41–59). Binghamton, New York: Haworth Press.

Walrond-Skinner, S. (1989). Spiritual dimensions and religious beliefs in family therapy. *Journal of Family Therapy, 11,* 47–67.

Walsh, F. (1999). Opening family therapy to spirituality. In F. Walsh (Ed.), *Spirituality resources in family therapy* (pp. 28–58). New York: Guilford Press.

Walsh, F. (Ed.) (1999). *Spirituality resources in family therapy*. New York: Guilford Press.

Walter, S. (1994). Does a systemic therapist have Buddha Nature? *Journal of Systemic Therapies, 13*(3), 42–49.

Warfield, R. D. (1996). Spirituality: The key to recovery from alcoholism. *Counseling and Values, 40*(3), 196–205.

Watts, A. (1961). *Psychotherapy east and west*. New York: Random House.

Welwood, J. (Ed.) (1983). *Awakening the heart: East/west approaches to psychotherapy and the healing relationship*. Boulder, CO: New Science Library.

Wheat, L. W. (1991). Development of a scale for the measurement of human spirituality (measurement scale). *Dissertation Abstracts International, 52*(09A), 3230.

Whitfield, C. L. (1984). Stress management and spirituality during recovery: A transpersonal approach. *Alcoholism Treatment Quarterly, 1*(1), 3–54.

Whyte, D. (1989–96). *The poetry of self-compassion* (audiotape). Langley, WA: Many Rivers Press.

Witvliet, C. V. O., Ludwig, T. E., & VanderLaan, K. L. (2001). Granting forgiveness or harboring grudges: Implications for emotions, physiology, and health. *Psychological Science, 12*, 117–123.

Wolf, C., & Stevens, P. (2001). Integrating religion and spirituality in marriage and family counseling. *Counseling and Values, 46*(1), 66–76.

Young-Eisendrath, P., & Miller, M. E. (Eds.) (2000). *The psychology of mature spirituality: Integrity, wisdom, transcendence*. Philadelphia, PA: Brunner-Routledge.

Zohar, D., & Marshall, I. (2000). *SQ: Spiritual intelligence: The ultimate intelligence*. New York: Bloomsbury.

Zumeta, Z. (1993). Spirituality and mediation, beyond technique: The soul of family mediation. *Mediation Quarterly, 11*(1), 25–38.

Some Web sites to visit for updates and more information:

Duke University Medical Center's Center for Spirituality,
Theology, and Health: http://www.dukespiritualityandhealth.org

http://www.SpiritResearch.org

Association for Transpersonal Psychology: http://www.atpweb.org

Bowling Green State University Psychology Department
Spirituality and Psychology Research Tea:
http://www.bgsu.edu/departments/psych/Facultyprograms.html/
SPIRIT.htm

International Center for the Integration of Health and Spirituality:
http://www.nihr.org

Bibliography

Assagioli, R. (2000). *Psychosynthesis: A collection of basic writings.* Amherst, MA: Synthesis Center.

Berland, W. (1998). *Out of the box for life.* New York: HarperCollins.

Bernard Shaw, G. (2001). *Man and superman.* New York: Penguin Classics.

Brown, S. (2003). Providing social support may be more beneficial than receiving it: Results from a prospective study of mortality. *Psychological Science.*

Buber, M. (1971). *I and thou.* New York: Touchstone.

Burns, G. (1998). *Nature-guided therapy.* Philadelphia: Taylor and Francis.

Campbell, J., with Moyers, B. (1988). *The power of myth.* New York: Doubleday.

Carlson, T., Kirkpatrick, D., Hecker L., & Killmer, M. (2002). Religion, spirituality, and marriage and family therapy: A study of family therapists' beliefs about the appropriateness of addressing religious and spiritual issues in therapy. *American Journal of Family Therapy*, *30*(2).

Coben, H. (2001). *Tell no one.* London: Orion Books.

Collins, J. (2001). *Good to great.* New York: HarperCollins.

DeLillo, D. (1998). *Underworld: A novel.* New York: Scribner.

Executive Speaker (2005). Exexcutive-Speaker.com. Quotations.

Frank, A. (1998). Just listening: Narrative and deep illness. *Families, Systems and Health*, *16*(3), 197–212.

Frankl, V. (1997). *Man's search for meaning.* New York: Pocket.

Frankl, V. (2000). *Recollections: An autobiography*. New York: Perseus.

Freud, S. (1927/1961). *The future of an illusion.* New York: W. W. Norton & Company.

Frumkin, H. (2001). Beyond toxicity: The greening of environmental health. *American Journal of Preventative Medicine*, *20*(3).

Gallup, G., Jr. (1998). *The gallup poll, public opinion 1997.* Wilmington, DE: Scholarly Resources, Inc.

Gilligan, S. (1997). *The courage to love.* New York: W. W. Norton & Company.

Glenn, S. (1989). *Developing capable people.* Provo, UT: Sunrise.

Gross, T. (2004). Fresh Air: Interview with Patsy Rodenberg. NPR.

Harris, K. (2005). *20th-century quotations*. Internet website. www.quotationspage.com

Johnson, F. (2003). *Keeping faith: A skeptic's journey*. New York: Houghton Mifflin.

Jung, Carl G. (1955). *Modern man in search of a soul.* New York: Harvest/HBJ.

Kleinman, A. (1988). *The illness narratives: Suffering, healing, and the human condition.* New York: Basic Books.

Koenig, H. G., McCullough, M. E., & Larson, D. B. (2001). *Handbook of Religion and Health*. Oxford, UK: Oxford University Press.

Kushner, H. S. (1981). *When bad things happen to good people.* New York: Avon.

Levin, J. (2001). *God, faith, and health: Exploring the spirituality-healing connection.* New York: Wiley.

Madanes, C. (1990). *Sex, love and violence.* New York: W. W. Norton & Company.

Mallinckrodt, B. (1996). Change in working alliance, social support, and psychological symptoms in brief therapy. *Journal of Counseling Psychology, 43*(4), 448–455.

Mills, J., Crowley, R., & Ryan, M. (1986/2001). *Therapeutic metaphors for children and the child within.* Philadelphia: Brunner-Routledge.

Neelman, J., & King, M. B. (1993). Psychiatrists' religious attitudes in relation to their clinical practice: A survey of 231 psychiatrists. *Acta Psychiatrica Scandinavica, 88,* 420–424.

O'Hanlon, B. (2000). *Do One Thing Different.* New York: Harper/Quill.

O'Hanlon, B. (2003). *A guide to inclusive therapy.* New York: W. W. Norton & Company.

Pargament, K. I., Smith, B. W., Koenig, H. G., & Perez, L. (1998). Patterns of positive and negative religious coping with major life stressors. *Journal for the Scientific Study of Religion, 37,* 710–724.

Paul, P. (2005). With God as my shrink. *Psychology Today*, May/June, pp. 63–68.

Smith, H. (2001). Letters from the heart. *Spirituality and Health,* spring.

Spirituality and Health (April, 2000). Survey on spiritual and religious beliefs of Americans.

Taffel, R., & Blau, M. (2002). *The second family: Dealing with peer power, pop culture, the wall of silence, and other challenges of raising today's teens.* New York: St. Martin's Griffin.

Weil, S. (1991). *Waiting for God*. San Bernadino, CA: Borgo Press.

Williamson, M. (1996). *A return to love*. New York: HarperCollins.

Whitaker, C. (2001). Personal communication.

Whitman, W. (2001). *Song of myself*. New York: Dover.

Whitney, C. (1999). Seeking the treads on stairway to faith. *USA Today*. McLean, VA: June 3, 1999. p. 15A.

Whyte, D. (1995). The poetry of self-compassion (audio tape). Whidbey Island, WA: Many Rivers Press.

Witvliet, C. V. O., Ludwig, T. E., & VanderLaan, K. L. (2001). Granting forgiveness or harboring grudges: Implications for emotions, physiology, and health. *Psychological Science, 12*, 117–123.

Worthington, E. L., Jr. (1998). Dimensions of forgiveness: Psychological research and theological perspectives. Philadelphia: Templeton Foundation Press.

Index